BLACK LANGUAGE STYLE IN SACRED AND SECULAR CONTEXTS

Carol Tomlin

Printed and published by
Caribbean Diaspora Press, Inc
At Caribbean Research Center
Medgar Evers College (CUNY)
1150 Carroll Street
Brooklyn, New York 11225
United States of America

Telephone: (718) 270 6082/6081
Fax   (718) 778 8306

Email: crc@ndl.net
www.ndl.net/~ny/crc

Library of Congress Catalog Card Number   99 076335

ISBN 1-878433-22-9

FOREWORD

This book is the <u>Tenth</u> in the Education and Culture series of the Caribbean Diaspora Press. It is the second that looks specifically at language issues among Caribbean speakers of Creole languages. It follows the work of Velma Pollard - <u>From Creole to Standard English</u> published in <u>1993.</u> Whereas Pollard addresses pedagogical strategies in Caribbean classrooms, Tomlin examinines the sociolinguistic reality of Caribbean immigrants in Britain, Particularly in religious and secular contexts.

Post-colonial debates have generated a great deal of interest in questions of language, culture and national identity, not only in the Third World, but also in metropolitan centers where there are large concentrations of Caribbean and African immigrants. In fact, the question of language and identity lies at the core of cultural nationalism worldwide. Notions of "nation language", Creole, Ebonics, and Black English have engaged scholars across the Caribbean, the U.S., Canada and Great Britain for decades.

Yet, mainstream society and policy makers have not yet resolved the ambivalences and insecurities involved in discussions of the validity and acceptability of Creole languages as mediums of communication and instruction or as indicators of authentic identity. Tomlin's work comes as a new contribution to the body of scholarly work that documents, analyzes and reiterates the intrinsic value of any vernacular, and the dynamic power of popular language as a social, cultural and political phenomenon.

Dr. J.A. George Irish

PREFACE

When did my fascination for the Black Language begin? You could say that it started when I was five years old in Britain in a South Yorkshire town called Doncaster, my birthplace. I remember visiting my relatives' house where the atmosphere was, as usual, exciting and electrifying and where the adults spoke Jamaican Creole. I distinctly remember the Jamaican records that were played. One in particular was a song with the following words: "Wat is quatty big bway ask? Wat is quatty? I want to know what is the show wat is quatty?" I am not sure of the exact words but throughout my life I have carried the memory of that song and I also remember rolling around in peels of laughter whenever that record was played.

The next turning point in my interest for the Language occurred when I was about 10 years old. By this time my family had relocated and settled in the city of Leeds, West Yorkshire. I attended and subsequently became a member of the New Testament Church of God, a Black Pentecostal church. Reflecting on my years as a young child I have tried to analyze the reasons why I behaved appropriately in Sunday School and always gained awards for being the best Sunday School student but how, this was not matched with my behavior and success in school. I was sometimes mischievous and a little disruptive in school and would often talk and 'have a laugh' with many of my peers. However, when I became a born again Christian the situation was rectified! I recall enjoying the activities at church. Everyone was the same color as myself and there was a natural affinity and rapport. Amazingly, I was able to sit still for an hour and listen to the most eloquent sermons. I was spellbound by the preaching of Pastor T. Caine and other preachers who came for the district conventions and building programs (a fundraising activity).

To this day, I am mesmerized by the Black style of preaching. I believe that God had planted the seed of interest in Black preaching and language in my heart, soul and mind. This point will later be developed. Sufficient to say at this stage that, God often allows one to experience different situations in life's journey for his ultimate purpose and to fulfill one's destiny.

It is not coincidental that I am second generation African-Caribbean female born in Britain, whose parents, like so many, migrated from Jamaica during the 1950s. Perhaps as a quest for identity, I was instinctively drawn to my peers who were born in the Caribbean and spoke Creole. I along with my peers, acquired Creole speech from Caribbean born family members friends. Parents often attempted to enforce the usage of standard or local English speech patterns onto their offspring. Caribbean parents wanted their children to succeed in British society and they felt that acquisition of British English was paramount. This is discussed in greater detail in the contents of the book. Schools across British cities and towns in the 1960s and 1970s which witnessed widespread Caribbean settlement became a breeding ground for the use of Creole among African-Caribbean students. I actually learnt many Caribbean play songs from friends, newly arrived from the Caribbean. It is worthwhile mentioning at this point that during my extensive travels throughout the British Isles, I have found that young Black people are influenced by the speech patterns of their parental birthplace. My own observation is that the Black Language is still alive and well and will remain so for the new millennium and the foreseeable future.

My awareness of the Black Language as a unique form of communication developed because of my experiences at school, significantly my high school, Primrose Hill, a large comprehensive school in Leeds. All the teachers were white. It had an African-Caribbean population of approximately 60%. The origins of several Black students in the school reflected the composite nature of the adult Black population in Leeds, where the vast majority originate from St. Kitts and Nevis; this is unlike many other cities where the Jamaicans predominate. Most of the students at Primrose Hill, during that time, were bilingual. Invariably, they spoke with the local Leeds accent and tended to 'switch' to Kittitian Creole. Some, like myself were able to speak Jamaican Creole and others were able to speak both Creoles. A few who were born or had parents from Barbados spoke Barbadian Creole.

A considerable number of teachers at Primrose Hill became conversant with the Creole language used by the Black students. A tiny minority even acquired Kittitian Creole and often conversed with African-Caribbean students in their mother tongue. However, miscommunication between White teachers and Black students would sometimes transpire. I vividly recall an encounter with one of the teachers during a Home Economics class. The students were speaking Kittitian Creole. I asked the teacher if she understood what they were saying. She replied that " it sounds like gibberish to me". It is interesting to note that many of the African-Caribbean students, not only at Primrose Hill but elsewhere did not pass ordinary level English examinations, especially at the high school level.

I believe that my schooling had such a profound influence on me that it served as a springboard for my passion in the field of Black Language and its and relationship to pedagogy. I also feel that God had allowed me to experience my education in the British educational system so that I would be able to record and relate to some of the issues of our present young black people. I can look back and see how God had all the pieces of the jigsaw of my life and how he fitted them back together. God's plan for my academic career was evident from the start of my undergraduate studies.

As a student teacher, whilst undertaking research on the affects of creole on academic achievement, I came across Professor Viv Edwards' book on the subject. She is considered to be one of Britain's leading experts in the field of Black Language. I wrote to her and the rest they say is history. Not only did I become one of her research assistance for a study exploring language use among young Black people in Dudley, a large town located in the in the West Midlands, but she later became my advisor/supervisor for my Ph.D. The Ph.D was a culmination of both undergraduate **and** other graduate studies. My masters of philosophy degree was based on research on Black preaching style. This was the catalyst for further research on Black Language, which has now become the basis of this work. As I previously mentioned, God had planted the seed in my life and it has now germinated in the fon-n of this book.

I do not think it is incidental that the recent Ebonics debate became a hotbed of contention in the United States. Nor is it by chance that Caribbean people both in the Caribbean and across the United States have similar issues related to Black Language as their Caribbean counterparts in Britain. This book is, therefore, intended for teachers, academics and politicians and anyone interested in the common diasporic experiences of African heritage people. In broad terms it is a book that examines the power of language.

CONTENTS

CHAPTER 1

INTRODUCTION

ঙ ঙ ঙ

This is about the language of Black people in the African diaspora. It aims to identify the range of language behaviours fund in Black communities in the Caribbean, America and Britain. It focuses specifically on the notion that Black people in the diaspora have inherited the African oral tradition and that underlying elements of African culture and language are still very much in evidence. For this reason, the terms *Black culture* and *Black language* will be used generically throughout the study to refer to the language and culture of Black people in the various geographical locations.

The origins of this common linguistic cultural heritage lie in the system of slavery, the institution responsible for the spread of Africans in the New World. African slaves came mainly from West Africa. Over a thousand different languages were spoken. Villages and states developed with their own central system of government. There were many religions including Christianity and Islam, but most people had their own traditional religion which promoted a belief in some form of 'Supreme Being' or god, different spiritual forces and respect for dead ancestors (Rees & Sherwood 1992).

These marked differences in African societies have been cited to show the obstacles African slaves in the New world faced in maintaining many aspects of their traditional culture and languages. However, while there is a considerable degree of linguistic and cultural diversity throughout this region, there are also strong underlying similarities. Mbiti (1977:2), for instance, talks about the 'understanding, attitude of mind, logic and perception behind the manner in which African peoples think, act or speak in different situations of life'.

The Study of Black Language

There has been a long history of racist attitudes towards Black language which has manifested itself either in neglect of study or the promotion of 'pathological' arguments. Herskovits (1937), for example, reports that until the late 1930s, the most common theory put forward to explain African-American speech was that it was 'the blind groping of minds too primitive in modes of speech beyond their capabilities'. More recently, the same pathological framework is to be detected in the work of writers such as Bereiter & Engelmann (1966) who talk in terms of language deprivation.

Scholarly interest in Black language is a fairly recent phenomenon and developed in America in the 1960s when there was much concern in educational circles about the academic under-achievement of Black children. This, in turn, led to a great deal of interest on the part of sociolinguists in the speech of African-Americans (cf Shuy et al 1968; Labov 1969) and to the recognition of non-standard dialects of English as a legitimate object of study.

Of all the geographical contexts, writers have paid most attention to the oral culture of African-Americans. For intance, Niles (1985), Rosenberg (1988), and Mitchell (1970; 1990) examine the oral performances of African-American preachers. Abrahams (1970b; 1976) and Kochman (1972) describe speech events in secular contexts such as verbal duelling. Smitherman (1977) identifies verbal devices such as call-response, tonal semantics and repetition in sacred and secular contexts.

The work of American writers has proved highly influential and has helped to stimulate interest among scholars in the language of the Caribbean. While there had been a fairly long tradition of interest on the part of anthropologists (cf Herskovitz 1937), the 1960s marked the burgeoning of interest on the part of sociolinguists (see for example, Bailey 1966; Cassidy & Le Page 1967). More recently writers such as De Camp (1971), Alleyne (1980) and Christy (1990) have further examined the language situation in the Caribbean.

Scholarly interest in Black language in a British context arose somewhat later and in response to both the pioneering efforts of American sociolinguists and the work on Caribbean language. The main accounts to date are Edwards (1979; 1983; 1986), Sutcliffe (1982; 1992) and Sebba (1993).

Interestingly, Africa, the source of Black language in the diaspora, has received a disproportionately small amount of attention in the literature. In the main, this area has been studied by anthropologists, who as a group have tended to be more concerned with other aspects of social organisation and culture. Important contributions to this area have, however, been made by Albert (1964; 1972), Finnegan (1970; 1977; 1988), Dalphinis (1985; 1990) and Okpewho (1992).

Increasingly, scholars have viewed the study of Black language in both the Caribbean and America from the perspective of the 'ethnography of speaking' which focuses on language behaviours in context rather than descriptions of phonology, syntax and lexis. Hymes' work (1972:2) provides a useful framework for this approach:

> Ethnography of communication implies two characteristics that an adequate approach to the problem of language which engage anthropologists must have .. It must call attention to the need for fresh kinds of data to the need to investigate directly the use of language in contexts of situation so as to discern patterns proper to speech activity, patterns which escape separate studies of grammar, of personality, of religion, of kinship and the like, each abstracting from the patterning of speech activity as such into some other frame of reference. Secondly, such an approach cannot take linguistic

form, a given code, or speech itself, as frame of reference. It must take as context a community, investigating its communicative habits as a whole, so that any given use of channel and code takes its place as but part of the resources upon which the members of the community can draw.

Most important, this ethnographic approach also provides a very powerful means of understanding the social values of those communities and the social basis for linguistic variation (cf Reisman 1974; Abrahams 1989). Although common linguistic features will also be analysed, the main descriptive framework for the discussion of Black speech in this study will fall within the ethnography of speaking.

Black culture is characterised by a rich oral tradition. In many African societies, knowledge, attitudes and ideas are transmitted orally, not through the written word. This African tradition has been retained by Black people in the Caribbean, America and Britain. As Folb (1980: 90) points out:

> The oral tradition is still pervasive in Black culture. Because who you are (and very often how well you survive) depends so heavily on how well you talk, verbal dexterity is highly valued.

Orality also has a performative function. In Black culture, oral performance is central to sharing the community norms and values and is greatly valued. The oral performer also enjoys high status.

To understand the variety of 'communicative habits' of Black culture, the social context in which communication takes place is very relevant. In Black culture any social occasion is a platform for verbal interaction. The focus for my previous research has been the church (Sutcliffe & Tomlin 1986; Tomlin 1988). The wider study of Black speech events, however, has made it clear that the same stylistic features underlie the organisation of language behaviours in both sacred and secular contexts. The present study therefore reflects this broadening of interests.

Notable speech events takes place in the home, on the street, in the club or in the church.

The study of Black speech has two dimensions: the linguistic which examines areas such as lexis, phonology, syntax and semantics, and the stylistic which examines the ways in which these different elements are combined to create a variety of effects. The two will be separated for the purposes of analysis although there are points of overlaps. This thesis first describes the linguistic features of Black speech in the diaspora and second identifies the range of stylistic features found in Africa which have been retained by Black people in the Caribbean, North America and Britain.

Its particular contribution is to document more fully the African dimension of Black speech in Britain. British research has focused very specifically on descriptive and educational issues and with the exception of Sutcliffe & Tomlin (1986) and Callender & Cameron (1990) who describe oratory in sacred settings, Sutcliffe (1982) who discusses Black oral narratives, and Edwards (1979; 1983) who briefly describes pre-adolescent verbal duelling, this research pays little attention to the exploration of speech events within the tradition of 'the ethnography of speaking'.

The Oral-Literate Continuum

As already mentioned, Black culture is essentially an oral one. A higher value is placed on the spoken rather than on the written word. However, literacy has had an enormous impact on Black communities throughout the world and it is within this context that the oral-literate continuum has to be examined in the present study.

The oral tradition is usually associated with cultures without writing, the literate tradition with societies where the development of writing has been intensified by the advent of print. Unfortunately, literates have often attached inferior status upon those who cannot read and write and illiteracy has come to be synonymous with ignorance. Equally misguided, however, is the view of the oral world as an unblemished expression of pure nature and where exponents of this view express a desire for a return to a preliterate world. In his work on the oral songs of Yugoslav epic singers, Lord (1960), for instance, illustrates the second of these two views. For Lord literacy poses an internal rather than external threat to orality. His concerns are not about the distortion of the oral experience through transcription but about the permanent change of the oral performer's skills.

Such a view is unduly pessimistic. Most writers today subscribe to the notion of an oral-literate continuum rather than discrete oral and literate states or entities. As Edwards and Sienkewicz (1990: 6) explain:

> The written word does not divide so much as the spoken word unites the alliterate and the literate; that is the presence of literacy does not remove all traces of orality nor must an oral culture always function independently.

Many cultural experiences bear this out. The idea still persists that new media are driving out older and established ones. For example, electronic media like the television are seen as replacing the print media of newspapers and books. Ong (1978) has described this phenomenon as secondary orality, to differentiate it from the primary orality of a culture unaffected by literacy. The sermon of the African-American preacher is a specific example of such secondary orality. The preacher is dependent on the literate culture of the written form, the Bible; at the same time he uses the strategies of oral culture to communicate the message.

In practice in most cultures, a mixture of orality and literacy is far more typical than a reliance on just one, with writing being used for some purposes and oral forms for others. The normality of mixed oral and literate modes in the history of traditional societies such as Asia and Africa is widely documented (cf Goody 1968). In West Africa, for example, a literate Islamic culture has developed alongside oral traditions. Islam is evident in the oral epic of Sunjata whose genealogy is often linked with the prophet Mohammed and his companions. The literate tradition does not replace the oral one. But, when literacy is introduced the two are intertwined with each other. Similarly, no individual is either 'oral' or 'literate' (Tannen 1988: 3).

Heath (1988: 111), for instance, provides clear evidence for the striking overlap between oral and literate traditions by examining the oral and literate patterns in Tracton a working class all-Black community in America. She argues that in Tracton the community is not on a continuum from full literacy to restricted literacy but, as she says `it seems more appropriate to think of two continua, the oral and the written`. In this community formal reading and writing is re-negotiated into an informal style which leads to discussion and debate among several people. Their knowledge is acquired from the text through the 'joint oral negotiation of meaning'.

However, different cultures lay different emphases on literacy and the specific use of oral media vary at different times and places. As Finnegan (1988: 175) says:

> Orality and literacy are not two separate and independent things...they take diverse forms in differing cultures and periods, are used differently in different social contexts and, insofar as they can be distinguished at all as separate modes rather than a continuum, they mutually interact and affect each other and the relationships between them are problematic rather than self-evident.

Data Collection
The present study is based on a number of sources in a variety of sacred and secular settings including published sources, literary accounts, audio-visual sources, the ESRC project, 'Patterns of language use in a British Black community' and speech recorded as part of the research for my M. Phil thesis on 'Black Preaching Style' (Tomlin 1988). Data from these sources have been obtained over a ten year period.

Published Sources

As mentioned above, Black language received very little scholarly attention for a long time. Writers like Herskovitz (1937) who studied folk speech in Surinam and Chandler (1918) who recorded Caribbean and American traditional narratives were very much the exception. It was not until the late 1960s that there was an explosion of interest in Black speech on the part of anthropologists and sociolinguists. Many accounts published in the last 30 years contain extensive transcripts and analyses of Black speech, particularly African-American speech. In providing an overview of the Black speech of the diaspora, these various sources were an obvious starting point.

In an American context, a number of writers have provided useful overviews and examples of African-American speech events, most notably Smitherman (1977) and Abrahams (1976). Rosenberg (1988) is a particularly rich source for the oral performance of African-American preachers, while Labov (1972) and Erickson (1984) offer examples and analysis of adolescent speech.

Published discussions of speech contexts outside America are more limited. Abrahams, the anthropologist who has studied a range of African-American speech events referred to above, has also provided in-depth discussion of comparable Caribbean data (Abrahams 1967; 1970; 1972c). Crowley (1966), Barrett (1976) and Tanna (1984) are excellent sources of data for story-telling performances.

The most important descriptions of African speech events are contained in Finnegan (1970; 1977; 1988) and Okpewho (1992); Cosentino (1982) also offers extensive examples and useful commentary on storytelling among the Mende in Sierre Leone.

Published transcripts of British Black speech events are very limited. However, Sutcliffe (1982) offers a range of oral narratives on which I draw; similarly Edwards (1983) includes examples of pre-adolescent verbal duelling.

Literary Sources

The debate on the extent to which literary sources reflect the linguistic reality of a speech community is relevant to the current study. Linguists have often rejected literary dialects as a reliable source of data because they are based on the work of the creative imagination. Petyt (1970), however, shows that Emily Bronte's portrayal of Haworth speech is very close to contemporary sources. Macaffee (1982) assumes that representations of Glaswegian speech by Glaswegian authors are accurate. Sullivan (1980) makes a powerful case for the authenticity of Hiberno-Irish speech in works of literature. Edwards et al (1984) also endorse the use of literary sources for study in an overview of research on the grammar of English dialect. In my own experience, as a speaker of Jamaican Creole, many Caribbean writers also represent local speech accurately in their work.

Very limited use is made of literary sources in the present work. However, on two occasions I made use of *The Ragdoll* by the Jamaican writer Hazel Campbell and the poem *Candy seller* by the poet Louise Bennett to draw attention to the very distinct patterns of oral language which are mirrored faithfully even in the written word.

Records

Most accounts of language draw exclusively on speech data rather than song. However, many of the characteristics of Black speech are especially evident in musical contexts, including call and response (as discussed in chapter 6) and repetition (as discussed in chapter 7). Gospel, reggae, rap and other contemporary records are another valuable source of data for the present study.

The popular West African gospel chorus *Highter Higher* and Jamaican reggae songs *Girlie Girlie* by Sopia George and *No woman no cry* by Bob Marley were chosen to illustrate the high degree or repetition found in Black speech. *Shut um down* by the African-American Rap Group, Public Enemy, *Tramps* by Salt 'N Pepper, an African-American female group and *Don Dadda* by Supercat were chosen because of their political messages. Other records, including the South African song *the digger* by Ipi 'N

Tombia and Margaret Singana and, Black British songs *My woman* by Force and *Don't turn Around* by Aswad, were used because they show important stylistic features of Black speech.

Audio/Video Sources

In a similar vein, professionally produced audio tapes of sermons by Dr Reverend Ben Idahosa and Dr Reverend Christ Tunde Joda from Nigeria, Reverend Blair from Jamaica, Pastor Ulrich from Antigua and Dr Martin Luther King from America were important sources of language in sacred settings in a variety of Black communities. I also obtained professionally produced video recordings of the sermons of Reverend Blair from Jamaica and Reverend Joel Edwards from Britain and an address by Reverend Joel Edwards at the wedding of Dawn and Ian Lewinson in Willesden.

I recorded the poem of Martin Glyn at St Anthony's College, Oxford. I also recorded the political speeches of Reverend Jesse Jackson at the Hackney Empire in London and Reverend Hewie Andrews at the Mary Moore School in Lambeth London. Both speeches provided good examples of the dynamic style of Black public speakers.

Original Material

These various sources have been supplemented by a large volume of material which I have collected myself - or helped to collect - over the last ten years based, mainly in Dudley, West Midlands. This material can be divided into two main categories: data collected as part of the ESRC project, 'Patterns of language use in a British Black community'; and data collected for an M Phil study of 'Black preaching style' (Tomlin 1988).

Collecting the Data

Many procedures are available for collecting original speech data about language. They range from a carefully planned intensive field investigation in a different country to introspection about one's mother tongue carried out at home. Hammersley & Atkinson (1987: 16) argue that ultimately all social research takes the form of participant observation in that it involves taking part in the social world and reflecting on the products of that participation. Junker (1960) and Gold (1958) outline a number of different observer roles: complete participant, participant as observer, observer as participant and complete observer. For the purposes of original data collection I was either a complete participant or an observer as participant.

Much of the original data was tape recorded. This enabled the claims that I made about the language to be checked and provided a way of ensuring that those claims were accurate. Obtaining natural and good-quality data is often difficult. People talk in a stilted fashion when they know they are being recorded, and the sound quality can be poor. However, a variety of tape-recording procedures have been devised to reduce the effects of what Labov (1968) has termed the 'observer's paradox', created when researchers observe the behaviour of people who know they are being observed. The problem of the observer's paradox has been approached in many ways. Gal (1979), for instance, spent a period of twelve months living as a member of the Oberwart community on the Austro-Hungarian border. Milroy (1980) gained access to Belfast speech by using network relations and introducing herself as a 'friend of a friend'. In return for spending time recording conversations in people's homes she participated in the life of the community, helping people out, for instance, by offering the use of her transport.

In some situations, other constraints, such as the sex or ethnicity of the researcher, will make it very difficult to achieve acceptance by members of the group. While it is possible to obtain genuine data based on vernacular speech or culture in inter-racial settings, a lot of time needs to be spent establishing credentials; this approach also requires a great deal of sensitivity.

The insider has obvious advantages over the outsider in gaining access to authentic language behaviour in a wide range of situations. Labov et al's (1968) Harlem project, for instance, made an important methodological innovation by combining the insights of professional linguists with insiders' knowledge of African-American language. I was an insider and one of the

11

several field workers for a research project on Black British Language based in Dudley, West Midlands, in the summer of 1982. The major findings have been published in Edwards (1986) and Sutcliffe (1992). The aim of the project was to document the patterns of language use among Black British young people. It drew on the speech of 45 young people. They were recorded in five different situations in single sex friendship groups of two or three in an attempt to explore the full range of their linguistic repertoires: a formal interview where the interviewer was White; a formal interview where the interviewer was Black; racially mixed informal conversation; Black informal conversation with field worker and Black peer group speech without the presence of a field worker. These situations thus varied considerably in their levels of formality. As one of two Black interviewers, I was responsible for both the formal interview and the informal discussion with the female participants. A second Black field worker, Leighton Bruce, was responsible for these same situations with the male participants.

It is important to note, however, that while, as a Black person I was clearly an insider in this data collection exercise, racial identity is not sufficient in itself to ensure access to authentic speech. In the pilot for the ESRC study, I found it impossible to elicit extended examples of vernacular speech, particularly in mixed sex conversation and, for this reason, in the main study I worked only with female respondents. In this situation, Black field workers have a considerable advantage over White field workers, but successful recording of authentic vernacular speech requires the establishment of genuine social relationships and the creation of realistic speech situations, irrespective of ethnic identity. It was necessary to look at variables such as situation, topic and composition of the group to ensure the production of vernacular speech.

The other material which I have collected relates to a study of Black preaching styles, based on two Black-led Pentecostal churches in Dudley, West Midlands: The New Testament Church of God and the First United Apostolic Church of Jesus Christ. Both churches have overwhelmingly working class Jamaican congregations. I informed both Pastor Jackson from the New Testament Church and Pastor Peter King from the First United Church that I was doing a study on Black preaching style and would need to tape some of their services. There was no objection to this in either church.

As an active member of the New Testament Church I had established my credibility. A few of my relatives were members of the First United Church and I already knew several members on a social level, so I was warmly received. Taping the services is a regular occurrence and, as an insider, I knew my presence would not affect the format of the services in any way. In 1985, over a six month period, I made several tape recordings of Sunday morning and evening services. The services included sermons, testimonies, prayers and songs. I also visited other Black-led Pentecostal churches in Leeds, Birmingham, Wolverhampton and London.

Structure of the Book
This book falls into *two main parts*. The *first part* sets the scene. Chapter two examines slavery and describes the social, historical and political development of Africans in the diaspora focusing on the Caribbean, North America and Britain. It explores the diversity of Black communities in these geographical locations and the different ways in which they have responded to their common experience of oppression.

Chapter three explores the language of Black people in the Caribbean, America and Britain and examines the historical events which led to their development. Attention is drawn to the many similarities between the structures of geographically dispersed varieties of Black language. Particular emphasis is also placed on attitudes towards Black language and the role these have played both in maintaining features of Black speech and in contributing to the academic under-achievement of Black children.

The *second part of this book examines the performative aspects of Black speech.* Chapters four and five describe the extensive range of speech events in Black communities throughout the world and provides the backdrop for the analysis of selected stylistic features which follows in subsequent chapters. Chapter four considers bad talk, such as verbal duelling and rapping, which explores the limits of accepted community values; while chapter five examines sweet talk, such as sermons and storytelling, which serves to reinforce friendship and community bonds.

Chapter six considers call-response, a basic characteristic of African communication in which an audience either echoes or adds to the utterance of a performer. It draws on evidence of highly stylised call-response behaviour of Black communities in Africa and the diaspora in both sacred and secular contexts. It examines a variety of call-response forms, such as co-signing, On T, encourager and repetition and, their various functions.

Chapter seven describes the use of repetition in a variety of Black speech contexts. It outlines specific examples from both sacred and secular domains including informal conversation, political speeches, sermons and music. The different forms of repetition such as simple repetition and near repetition and the various functions which they serve such as reinforcing shared group values and creating dramatic effect, are examined.

Chapter eight presents the conclusions which emerge from the study. It considers the implications of cross-cultural communication for Black and White speakers in a variety of social and educational settings, and indicates directions for future research.

CHAPTER 2

THE AFRICAN DIASPORA

ଃ ଃ ଃ

This chapter will deal with the historical, social, economic, and political forces on Africans in the diaspora focussing on the Caribbean, North America and, in particular, Britain. In order to understand the African diaspora it is essential to look first at the African homeland. Attention will be paid to slavery, the main institution responsible for the spread of Africans and African culture into the New World. We will examine the political and socio-economic development of Black people in the Caribbean and America during slavery and in the post-emancipation period. Attention will be placed on Black people in Britain focussing on post-war migration from the Caribbean and their response to racism in the areas of housing and employment.

Throughout this chapter we will consider the various institutions and the role they have played in transmitting and imposing White culture, especially education. We will look at the achievement levels of Black students in the various geographical locations. Emphasis will also be placed on Black religious life, one of the strongest areas of African retention. An examination of these areas and the ways in which Black people have resisted the forces of oppression is necessary to provide a backdrop for the discussion of Black language which follows in subsequent chapters.

The African Homeland

We shall be arguing throughout this book that underlying elements of African culture and language are still very much in evidence in the African diaspora. This might suggest an over simplistic view of Africa. It is certainly the case that the areas of West Africa, the source of the diaspora, are extremely diverse. Thousands of years saw the evolution of many different societies, with many different kinds of political organisations, many different languages (for further discussion, see chapter three) and many different religions (Rees & Sherwood 1992).

Yet in spite of the fact that West African societies were so heterogeneous, there were also very many underlying similarities, which Redfield (1953: cited in Levine 1977: 4) chooses to discuss under the umbrella of 'style of life'. He points out, for instance, that different groups of people from the same regions with diverse languages, religions and institutions may still share certain morals, ideals and general ways of looking upon the world. Levine (1977:4-5) offers a similar argument:

> Though they varied widely in language, institutions, gods, and familial patterns, they shared a fundamental outlook toward the past, present, and future and common means of cultural expression which could well have constituted the basis of a sense of common identity and world view capable of withstanding the impact of slavery. We must be sensitive to the ways in which the African world view interacted with that of the Euro-American world into which it was carried.

Slavery

Another factor which has had a profound effect in moulding the African diaspora has been the common experience of oppression by Whites. The diaspora was brought about by the introduction of slavery into the Americas by Christopher Columbus in the fifteenth century. Interestingly, however, Africa was not the first port of call in the slave trade. The Carib and Arawak Indians were, in fact, the first group of people in the Caribbean to be systematically enslaved and forced to work on the crop plantations. This use of enforced labour increased with the

16

Spanish Conquest of the New World. The Indians, especially the Caribs, made every effort to resist the European invasion. They fought fiercely against the Spanish but their weapons were ineffective. In spite of the 1542 Laws of the Indies which decreed that the Indians were free people, the use of compulsory labour continued in Hispanic America. In many areas of the New World the indigenous populations were unable to adjust to the rigid and rigorous requirements of enforced labour; they almost disappeared as a result of hard work, disease and malnutrition (Foner 1976).

In many European territories in the New World, particularly the British West Indies and North American colonies, the immediate successors of the indigenous slaves were the landless poor Whites, indentured servants, deported criminals and political prisoners, and religious refugees from various part of Europe. However, they could not fulfil the labour demands of the plantations and European traders turned to Africa for slaves to fill the gap. Although there is evidence of an African presence in the Americas in the fifteenth century, their status is unclear (Lawrence 1962). Nicolas De Ovande, governor of Hispaniola, was in fact the first to introduce African slaves in 1502, thus initiating a trade which ultimately brought millions of Africans to the New World.

This slave trade is associated in many minds with the famous Atlantic triangle, the route taken by slave ships. It was dominated by the British who sold slaves to other European countries with colonies in the Caribbean. On leaving Britain, the slave ships sailed to the west coast of Africa. Africans were then captured and forced to march to coastal forts where they were imprisoned. The trade involved the barter with many African chiefs of manufactured goods for slaves; these, in turn, were sold in the West Indies in exchange for sugar or bills of exchange payable in England. An important part of this process was the so-called 'Middle Passage', the horrendous journey from Africa to the West Indies or the North American mainland during which large numbers of slaves perished.

African-Caribbeans

Between 1620 and 1650 the English, Dutch and French all established colonies in the Caribbean; the geography of the West Indies was in fact created by European rivalry. The subsequent development of the West Indies is inextricably bound with sugar and slavery. Sugar cultivation was introduced into these colonies during the seventeenth century and the Caribbean islands rapidly developed into large scale producers. Sugar was a commodity which was easy to produce and in great demand. However, it was also labour intensive. By the end of the eighteenth century, sugar plantations with large African slave work forces had spread to every Caribbean island (Lowenthal 1972).

The production of sugar created similar social structures and lifestyles throughout the Caribbean. Consequently, European settlers were able to move from one Caribbean island to another with relative ease. Similarly, slaves moved between territories as chattel, or to elude capture as runaways. The continuous flux of people created a common culture of ideas and institutions. Threats of slave uprisings, natural disasters or outside competition required a level of co-operation between islands. Formal inter-territorial organizations and informal transnational values played an important part in Caribbean affairs. In spite of territorial rivalry, there was overall unity.

The use of slavery in sugar production operated like a smoothly functioning machine making it possible for plantations to be run by absentee owners For example 60 per cent of Grenada's sugar estates, 80 per cent of those in St Vincent and Tobago and 90 per cent of cultivated land in Jamaica was owned by absentees. White skin was the main qualification for office (De Rueck et al 1967).

Slaves were seen primarily as property rather than as people. Their conditions and treatment varied according to the nationality and religion of the owner, the nature of the local economy and the numerical balance between Black and White. For the greatest part, however, slaves were treated brutally, dehumanized and underfed (Craton 1982).

West Indian slaves, however, could and did gain their freedom, especially if they were racially mixed, or coloured. West Indian White society tolerated free coloured people because they were needed in the occupational strata of society, for example as labourers, traders and in the militia. They were distinguishable from slaves not only by their freedom but by colour. West Indian Whites regarded free coloured people as superior both to slaves and free Blacks and they were given special privileges, although they none the less experienced discrimination (cf Patterson 1967). For example, in Jamaica 75 per cent of the free coloured were reputed to be poor. There was in fact much conflict between the free coloured and Whites. In the French Antilles, for example, White settlers resented free coloured privileges and wealth and imposed restrictions on their lifestyle and work (Lowenthal 1972).

Slavery ended as an institution as a result of many forces, including slave revolts, economic self-interest and humanitarian reform in England and America. Sugar was in decline in the West Indies, but, as we will see, the growth of the cotton industry in the United States gave slavery a sharper edge. Abolition became a moral issue and was championed by leading figures in Philadelphia and New York in America, and in London and Manchester in England (Craton 1982). In the Caribbean, slave revolts led by figures such as Toussaint L'Ouverture in San Domingo (now known as Haiti) and the Maroon Warrior Nanny in Jamaica also made an enormous impression on the anti-slavery movement. Slavery officially ended in the islands that belonged to the French in 1794 and in the British territories in 1838. The Virgin Islands owned by the Danes followed suit shortly afterwards, though, in Surinam, slavery did not end until 1873.

The Post-Emancipation Period
For most slaves, however, emancipation was partial and incomplete. They remained in a state of economic bondage, and political and social limbo (Lowenthal 1972). Planters and governments throughout the Caribbean curtailed the freedom of labourers binding them to the estate so as to increase sugar production; Whites still owned the best land. Where other crops such as, cotton, coconuts, coffee, cacao and bananas outlasted or

replaced sugar, however, Whites were less successful in preventing non-White acquisition of land. In the main, Blacks were forced to work for low wages or face hunger, eviction or imprisonment. Therefore, even though the plantation system had ended, many former slaves forsook the estates for small holdings. In Surinam, the Windward islands, Montserrat and Virgin Islands, former slaves rented land and worked it as sharecroppers.

To keep wages down and ensure a steady labour supply, sugar growers introduced Chinese and Madeiran indentured labourers. In the course of time, these newcomers left agriculture, entering the retail trade and also becoming peddlers. East Indians and Javanese were subsequently imported to work on the land. Indian indentured labourers endured particularly harsh conditions reminiscent of slavery. As the East Indian population increased in islands such as Trinidad, Blacks moved off the sugar estates into the towns or on to small holdings.

Most ex-slaves participated in local affairs only marginally more than East Indians. In the French and British Caribbean for instance, Whites controlled the local legislature with a handful of men of colour. The twentieth century, however, has witnessed a shift in power in the Caribbean. Blacks and other people of colour increased their influence in government and other institutions. None the less, the relationship between Blacks and Whites remains substantially unchanged.

In contrast with America, where civil war and great turmoil accompanied emancipation, plantocracy remained intact in the West Indies with little challenge to existing power structures and values. The continued separation of the Black majority from the White and Brown minorities meant the poor, who were mainly Blacks, developed their own patterns of behaviour and beliefs (cf Alleyne 1988).

Colour distinctions, between Whites, Browns and Blacks still persist in the Caribbean today. Even though Blacks have gained some positions of leadership, high status posts not held by whites remain a light-coloured domain. This tendency, however, has become less pronounced since the independence of most Caribbean islands. Non-Whites are in the majority in all government areas. They now occupy most places of public eminence, a development which has resulted in great changes in public attitudes.

Education

Education developed slowly in the Caribbean. West Indian Whites, like Europeans, thought schooling to be suitable only for the elite. Many of the elite were educated in Europe and the islands had only a very basic school system. Small education grants came from the metropolitan government and from churches; smaller sums came from local legislatures. Most schools catered to Whites alone; middle-class Brown skinned children later gained admission. Higher education was an elite process and based on the European model, designed to turn out gentlemen and administrators.

Primary and secondary schooling spread slowly and did not really affect the masses. Although primary education was compulsory, it was not universal. As late as the 1940s, one Caribbean person in three could not read or write, and one in four never attended school. Half the remainder attended irregularly and most received less than five years of schooling. Most primary schools involved rote learning and practical studies, ensuring that the lower classes would go into manual labour. The secondary school system catered for Whites unable to afford education abroad, and non-Whites on their way up the social ladder. The secondary school curriculum tended to be academic rather than practical. Until fairly recently both the primary and secondary school curriculum focused on Europe rather than the Caribbean and was geared to the various British General Certificate of Education examinations.

There have, however, been some significant changes in primary and secondary school curriculum. Much of the material in use in the primary school is now Caribbean in origin. There have been developments such as the University of the West Indies USAID Primary Education project which produced curriculum materials in the areas of language, arts and mathematics. The changes in the secondary school curriculum were brought about through the establishment of the Caribbean Examination Council (CXC) in 1979 which replaced the British General Certificate of Education examinations. The Council's syllabuses are designed to be relevant to Caribbean pupils (cf Murray & Gbedemah 1983).

In spite of the innovations in the curriculum, many problems remain. In Jamaica for example, education is not compulsory and, while 98 per cent of primary school age children are enrolled in school, regular attendance is approximately 65 per cent (Miller 1990). In some Caribbean islands such as Jamaica and the British Virgin Islands there is a problem of overcrowded classrooms (Smawfield 1990). Over the past 20 year strenuous efforts have been made to reduce overcrowding in primary schools.

Funding for education in many Caribbean islands is inadequate. Consequently, a large proportion of textbooks, workbooks and basic teaching apparatus and equipment are also purchased from funds which schools have raised themselves. Considerable responsibility is thus placed on schools and parents, but many parents are too poor to help (Smawfield 1990).

Religion
The main religion in the Caribbean is Christianity. Religious faith and practice differ according to social class throughout the Caribbean. The elite attend church as a religious duty and tend to belong to established churches such as Anglican or Methodist. Middle class Caribbean people also belong to various established denominations but take religion more seriously. Most working class people, however, attend fundamentalist churches such as the Seventh Day Adventist and Pentecostal (Lowenthal 1972: 114).

Syncretistic cults which bring together elements of African and European religious tradition, also have a working class following. We find, for instance, the Spiritual Shakers of St Vincent, the Baptist Shouters of Trinidad and the Pocomanias of Jamaica. These cults combine traditional, evangelical and fundamentalist forms of Christianity with revivalism and spiritualism. They believe both in salvation by faith and in a spirit world, where the dead have supernatural powers and mediate among the living. These cults also demand active congregational participation. Their worship generates intense emotion, often culminating in group induced spirit possession and public conversion.(cf Simpson 1978) Tracing the origins of these cults is extremely difficult and complicated. However, they have various historical antecedents. For example, in Jamaica, Revival, Revival Zion, Pocomania and Convince came from a revivalist movement initiated by 'Native Baptist' slaves. Whereas African retentions can be found in the belief systems of Vodun in Haiti or Pocomania in Jamaica, the African elements in other Caribbean belief systems among the working classes are much more tenuous.

The African belief in supernatural forces or witchcraft is also widespread among the working classes in the Caribbean. It has been suggested that witchcraft known as 'obeah' or 'jumbie' is an African retention (Barrett 1976). However, Beckwith (1929:84) argues that folk beliefs in Jamaica, for instance, 'differ in no way from European patterns and are most likely taken directly from the whites'. The De Laurence Company of Chicago, a white owned company, is the main Caribbean supplier of instructions and magic texts outlining sources of recipes for potions and formulae used to invoke supernatural powers. It is interesting to note that even the elite and middle classes, whilst denying any association with magic, in cases of mental breakdown often revert to magical practices and healing. As Morrish (1982: 42) explains:

Obeah still seems to permeate the whole social scale in Jamaica, although it is strongly condemned in public, and its practice is a serious criminal offence

Pentecostalism has also had a tremendous impact on the religious life of mainly working class people in the Caribbean. Azusa Street in Los Angeles is the accepted birthplace of the modern day Pentecostal movement, (cf Hollengweger 1972; Synan 1975) characterized by glossalia, (speaking in an unknown language), expressive and interactive worship and a fundamental belief in the Bible. Pentecostalism became the fastest growing religious movement in the Caribbean after the Second World War. Its growth has paralleled the decline in the syncretistic cults and historic denominations. As MacRoberts (1984:10) writes:

> Its phenomenal growth since the early 1950s has been largely under the leadership of indigenous ministers, many of whom were introduced to Pentecostalism while working in the States. They established indigenized Pentecostal sects which combined the status of Christian denomination with the popularity and spiritual power of the syncretistic ancestor, revivalist and Native Baptist cults. Pentecostalism, because of its syncretistic nature, was particularly amenable to indigenization.

In the Caribbean the working class and upper class faiths differ tremendously not only in the liturgical practices but also in patterns of worship. In the established churches worship is perhaps more subdued. However, in the various cults and Pentecostal churches, worship includes spirit possession, dancing and other motor behaviour like sudden 'jerking' or bouncing up and down which is essentially African (Herskovitz 1958).

African-Americans

The experiences of the African slaves in the Caribbean are similar to those in North America. The early history of Black people in America also involved colonisation by Europeans, and was greatly marked by the influence of Britain and the Atlantic slave trade. By the end of sixteenth century, the demand for cheap labour to exploit America's resources could no longer be satisfied by indentured servants from Europe. Slavery was first introduced in Virginia in 1619, but was not fully developed until some 70 years later.

By the eighteenth century the plantation system, based mainly on crops of tobacco, rice and indigo, was well established in the five southern English colonies, Maryland, Virginia, North Carolina, South Carolina and Georgia. Over 36 per cent of the population were African slaves, some 220,000 out of 609,000. There were field slaves, who worked on the land, domestics who worked in the plantation owner's house and skilled and semi-skilled craftsmen. Slaves in every Southern colony - whether field hands or domestics - were property and viewed as investment in capital, items of commercial exchange in the same way as animals.

There were many codes and repressive laws aimed at controlling slaves. For example, the 1705 Slave Code forbade assemblies among slaves and prohibited them from carrying any weapons or leaving plantations without the written permission of their masters. The punishments meted out were also severe. For petty offences, slaves were whipped, maimed or branded; for more serious crimes, they were hanged in a brutal manner. Slaves could buy their freedom but this was very difficult (Foner 1976).

As was the case in the Caribbean, the importance of slavery in the social and economic life of colonial America is clear, particularly in the south. However, it was by no means an exclusively southern phenomenon. In the northern cities, a small number of slaves served as domestic servants in the households of the upper classes. They also played a vital role in industry and commerce in cities such as of Philadelphia, although the importation of White indentured servants, mostly from Germany, and opposition from the Society of Friends meant that Black slaves were relatively few in number (cf McManus 1973).

Nor was slavery as deeply entrenched in the middle colonies and New England, as in the South. According to the censuses of 1755 and 1756, Blacks in Newport totalled 7 per cent of the population; in Boston they made up 8 per cent of the population; and in New York 16 per cent. In contrast, it is estimated that Blacks comprised 40 per cent of the population of Charleston, in the south. The predominantly mixed-farming economy in the north did not greatly encourage the large-scale employment of slave labour. Still, they performed a useful economic function as farm hands, domestic, skilled and unskilled labourers. Throughout the colonial period, from Delaware to Massachusetts, slave labour was widely used in agriculture, manufacturing, skilled crafts and in the home (Foner 1976).

The treatment of the slaves in the northern colonies was not as harsh as in the south, although it was harsher in the middle colonies than in New England. In New York and New Jersey, for example, the slave codes were particularly oppressive. These colonies were also the ones in which slavery was more important economically and which contained the largest number of slaves in proportion to the White population (McManus 1973).

In general, the status and treatment of the free Blacks in the northern colonies, as in the south, was between that of a slave and a free white person. At the end of their term of service, White indentured servants shared the same status as other free White men. However, free Blacks during this period shared only some of the rights or privileges of other free men. No distinction was made between Blacks and those who were racially mixed, known as mulattos. In all British colonies in America, it was held that "one drop of Negro blood makes a Negro". This position differed from the Spanish and Portuguese and French view which recognised a hundred and twenty shades of colour (Foner 1976). Racial classification in America was also different to the West Indies where elaborate racial terminology exists to describe different shades of colour (Patterson 1967).

As a consequence of their treatment and status, slaves often became fugitives and, according to reports from New England and Georgia, resistance was widespread. Runaways were a persistent problem in every colony. They included both acculturated slaves, ie those able to speak English, and those who had recently arrived from Africa. Those who fled from the south often found haven in the north and free Black communities emerged on a relatively small scale. As slavery was a feature of all the English colonies, the northern colonies afforded the fugitives only limited refuge and protection. Consequently, many runaways found a haven outside the English colonies, especially in Florida among the Spanish, who were enemies of the British, and among Native Americans (cf Bennett 1993).

Other forms of resistance included the refusal of newly imported slaves to acknowledge their familiarity with the use of certain tools that they had used in Africa, such as the hoe. Thus Dubois (1946, cited in Foner 1976: 265) suggests that African slaves "were the first in America to stage the 'sit-down' strike, to slow up and sabotage the work of the plantation". Arson, was another common form of resistance. Blacks set fires to ships, warehouses, barns and other buildings and, especially, to the homes of their masters. Poison was another method used by slaves who wanted revenge against the masters for their brutality. In 1748 the Virginia House of Burgesses passed a criminal statute making the practice of medicine by slaves punishable by death because poison had been substituted for medicines on too many occasions. The punishment meted out to slaves who committed such acts was barbaric: they were often roasted and burnt alive. The Boston Evening Post of 6th July, 1741, for instance, reports that: "Three Negroes have lately been burnt at Hackensack in New Jersey for burning of seven Barns". However, brutal punishment did not deter the slaves and there were many conspiracies and revolts. For example, the successful slave insurrection of 1712 in New York had repercussions all over the northern colonies for the following two decades (Foner 1976).

Black leaders such as Frederick Douglass and Harriet Tubman also played an important role in sharpening the anti-slavery debate, as did Quakers such as Benjamin Lay and John Woolman. The first abolitionist society was founded in 1775, headed by Benjamin Franklin, a former slave owner. However, it was the War of Independence which brought the matter to widespread attention. The emancipation of slaves began in the north without recourse to arms but required a civil war in the southern states before the issue was resolved. The legislation outlawing slavery was enacted in 1808 but this trade continued illegally for some fifty years.

The Post-Emancipation Period
At the end of the Civil War in 1865, the Thirteenth Amendment was added to the Constitution. This effectively ended slavery as a legal institution. The period following the Civil War, between 1865 and 1885, was an important turning point in the history of Black people in America. Reconstruction, the process of building

up the whole United States after the war, was resisted by many southern states. In the south, a series of very harsh codes to control the movement and activities of Black people were enacted. However, a Civil Rights Act in April 1866 guaranteed citizenship rights for slaves. In June 1866, the Fourteenth Amendment was passed which gave Black people equal voting rights. Again, it was resisted in the southern states and in 1867 Congress responded with the Construction Act, forcing the southern states to ratify the Fourteenth Amendment. During Reconstruction much progress was made towards making Black people full citizens. The Fifteenth Amendment of 1870 further secured equal voting rights for Black people. They were also elected to state legislative and other offices and made great social and political strides. Significantly, it was during this time that the Ku Klux Klan, known as the 'Invisible Empire', emerged.

The Post-Construction period soon followed in 1876. It marked the return of restrictions on civil liberties for Black people and lasted for another hundred years. It was a period of widespread discontent and political confusion. Many states, including the southern ones, gained 'States Rights', that is the rights of the state to control their own political affairs.

With States Rights in the south came the Jim Crow Laws, which had the effect of restricting the political and economic progress of Blacks. They were based on the notion of the races being separate but equal. There were no official Jim Crow Laws in the North but Black people still experienced racial discrimination.

The Twentieth Century
In the early twentieth century, groups of Blacks began to challenge the legal system that denied their civil liberties. For instance, the   National Association for the Advancement of Coloured People (NAACP) founded by WEB Du Bois in 1909, was at the centre of the struggle for social justice. Its efforts were complemented by such organisations as the National Urban League (Long 1985).

The First World War had a significant impact on African Americans. The labour demand created by war-time production in the industrial north sparked a massive migration from the south to the north. Blacks tended to settle in certain sections of the cities, later to be called ghettos. The majority of African- Americans, remained trapped by the same poverty and segregation they had known in the rural south and this became a political issue.

The democratic movement against US racial segregation in the 1930s and 1940s was determined by four main factors: firstly the election of Franklin D Roosevelt as President in 1932, and the shift in Black electoral allegiance from the Republican to the Democratic Party; secondly, the unprecedented crises in the domestic and world capitalist economies, leading to the Great Depression; thirdly, the rise of Fascism; and lastly the outbreak of the Second World War and the rise of militant trade unionism within America (Marable 1985).

The Great Depression of the 1930s, in particular, was even more devastating for Blacks already at the bottom of the social and economic ladder. Roosevelt's New Deal measures were designed to relieve the economic pressure in the country, but did not greatly enhance the position of the Black population as a whole. The most important priority for the New Deal was to submerge the civil rights issue in order to maintain greater party unity in the south. It therefore, had the effect of sustaining the structures of Jim Crow. (Marable 1985).

By the 1950s opposition to segregation in the south was gaining ground. The case of Brown vs the Boards of Education in 1954, ruled that separate educational facilities were 'inherently illegal', and reversed the decision of 1896 that had established the legal basis for the separate but equal dictum. In the face of White intransigence, Black groups formed to press for the elimination of segregation in the south .

During this time Martin Luther King Jr, the charismatic Black civil rights leader, emerged as an important political force, arguing for non-violent strategies to organise and mobilize Blacks into action which culminated in the famous march on Washington in 1963. Various Civil Rights Acts and the voting Rights Act of 1965 followed. Malcolm X, the Black muslim leader who, incidentally, opposed King, was also an important figure in the struggle for Black freedom during this period (Long 1985). The Black consciousness movement in the 1960s also had a significant impact on the progress of Black people.

Affirmative action or equal opportunity provisions in the private sector created new jobs for Black workers. Almost all public school systems were compelled to extend some measure of educational equality to Black youth. In the colleges and universities, Black enrolments soared from about 75,000 in 1950 to 666,000 by 1976. In the private sector, Black entrepreneurs promoted solid growth. In 1975 a third of all blacks were considered middle class (Marable 1985).

However, the social and economic gains which Blacks made began to wane by the 1980 By 1982, 20 per cent of all Black men (approximately two million) were out of the labour force, a 200 per cent increase from the 1970s. Over 50 per cent of all Black children were born out of wedlock and more than 60 per cent of these families lived in poverty. This represented a significant deterioration from the position in 1967 when almost six out of every ten Black families had two or more income earners and 75 per cent of all Black households had two parents (Marable 1985).

In the 1990s the situation appears even more bleak. Even though the laws have been changed to prevent discrimination, Black people are still at the bottom of the social, economic and political ladder. Black men, in particular, seem to be vulnerable. The average Black male is more likely to go to prison than university. His life expectancy is falling and he is seven times as likely to be murdered as a White male. In Washington DC nearly four times as many Black men were jailed in the district's prison as graduated from its public schools. In 1990, the unemployment rates among Blacks was 10.5 per cent, more than twice that for Whites. Over 34 per cent live below the poverty line (The Economist 1991a; 1991b).

Educational Under-Achievement

The experience of Black people in education is just as depressing as their social and economic situation. The under-performance of lower income Black children, in particular, has been and still is, cause for concern. A great deal of evidence exists to support the view that many Black children are underachieving in comparison to their White counterparts (Samdua 1975; Asamen 1989). Several factors have been put forward to account for their academic under-performance.

Black under-achievement has been explained in terms of Black intellectual inferiority. This position dates back to the days of slavery when Blacks were not educated because it was believed they were mentally deficient (Lieberson 1980). This view regained currency when the racial status quo was threatened during the Black Civil Rights Movement in the 1960s and the debate over desegregation of America schools resurfaced. Jensen (1969) restated the traditional views on genetic intellectual inferiority of Blacks to a barrage of criticism from many quarters (cf Jencks 1975).

By the 1970s the blame for educational failure had shifted from the intellectual abilities of Black children to the family and the notion of 'cultural deprivation'. It was alleged that Black children were linguistically and cognitively deficient, with a wide range of 'substandard' attitudes, norms and values. A series of compensatory education programmes were devised during the 1960s and early 1970s to make up for these deficits. However, the notion of cultural deprivation was challenged by a number of writers. Keddie (1973:8), for example, wrote:

> It appears therefore that the term became a euphemism for saying that working class and ethnic groups have cultures which are at least dissonant with, if not inferior to the 'mainstream' culture of the society at large. Culturally deprived children, then, come from homes where the mainstream values do not prevail and are therefore less

'educable' than other children. The argument is that the school's function is to transmit the mainstream values of society and the failure of children to acquire these values lies in their lack of educability. Thus their failure in school is located in the home, in the pre-school environment, and not with the nature and social organisation of the school which 'processes' the children into achievement rates.

It was further maintained that one of the consequences of living in a racist society was that children had a low self-esteem which could affect academic performance (cf Pettigrew 1964). This position has been widely criticised. The findings of numerous studies reviewed by Weinburg (1977) and Rosenberg (1979). point to little or no difference in self-concept between Black and White children.

The attention has shifted gradually from Black children and their families to schools and teachers. There is a legacy, for instance, of low expectation which may well influence teacher perception (cf Leacock 1971).

Religion
Religion, especially Christianity, is an important aspect of African-American culture. Most Blacks who profess religious affiliation are Baptists or Methodists. This reflects the fact that these two denominations were more active than others in converting Black slaves to Christianity, holding numerous revivals and camp meetings during the latter half of the eighteenth century and at the turn of the nineteenth century. In addition, the Baptist and Methodist churches had a greater degree of autonomy than churches in other denominations and it was easier for Blacks to become preachers and therefore leaders. The expressive style of worship found in these two churches at the time also appealed to many Blacks (cf Hamilton 1972).

Many independent Black churches were founded in the late eighteenth and early nineteenth century because of racial discrimination. Blacks were excluded from voting in mixed churches and were usually assigned to a remote corner of the gallery. For instance, the first Independent Black church, the African Methodist Episcopal church was established by Richard Allen as a result of separate seating arrangements between Blacks and Whites (cf George 1973).

It is a commonly held view that one of the strongest areas of African retentions is in the Black religious experience and expression (cf Herskovits 1958; Simpson 1978). Black religious life is usually characterised by its high level of emotion. The religious hysteria or spirit possession popularly known as 'shouting', 'getting happy' or 'getting the spirit' observed in certain Black churches has been variously attributed to residues of African culture, innate primitive emotionalism and the emotionalism of the uneducated masses. Emotional levels, however, seem to be loosely related to social position and the particular churches to which Black people belong. Not all Black church goers exhibit the same degree or type of demonstrative behaviours.

Several writers have commented on the key role that the Black church has played in the struggles of Black people (Wilmore 1989; Lincoln & Lawrence 1990). Black churches, particularly Black preachers have been directly involved in every movement connected with the liberation of Black people. In the days of slavery, for instance, there were some preachers such as Richard Allen who repudiated slavery but were not revolutionary and others like Reverend Nat Turner who felt commanded by God to lead a violent revolt against slavery. In more recent times, church leaders have become involved in social, economic and political issues. for example, the South Christian Leadership Conference (SCLC) led by the late Dr Martin Luther King was instrumental in several mass protest demonstrations on civil rights issues in the late 1950s and early 1960s (Hamilton 1972).

In response to the Black Power Movement in 1966 Black clergy from virtually every denomination began to reassess the relationship of the Christian church and the Black community. Out of this re-examination a 'Black theology' developed emphasising the role of the church as a means of liberating people from oppressive social, political and economic systems. Jesus is seen as Black and a revolutionary and 'the gospel of Christ is pre-eminently the gospel of the liberation of the oppressed' (Cone 1970: 23).

Another major religious movement that has had a considerable influence on African-Americans is the Nation of Islam (Black Muslims). Its followers believe that Allah (God) appeared in Detroit in July 1930 in the person of Mr W. Fard Muhammed. His mission was to achieve freedom, justice and equality for all the Black people of North America. He organised a temple which grew rapidly and a following committed to separatism: "We believe that it is the time for the separation of the -called Negroes and the so called White Americans ".(cited in Hamilton 1972: 81)

The growth of the Nation of Islam coincided with the rise of the Black Power Movement. During that time, the most prominent spokesman for the Muslims was Malcolm X, who eventually departed from the group to form his own organisations, the Muslim Mosque and the Organisation of Afro-American Unity (Hamilton 1972).Today the Nation of Islam is under the leadership of Louis Farrakhan and is actively engaged in uplifting the social and economic conditions of the Black family (*Ebony* 1993: 100).

British Blacks
We now turn our attention to Black people in Britain. Their situation reflects a combination of features from both the Caribbean on the one hand and America on the other hand. British Blacks come in the main from the Caribbean where they have formed part of the ethnic majority population. In Britain, however, they form a small but significant Black minority which is more reminiscent of America than the Caribbean.

Small numbers of Africans have been in Britain since Elizabethan times but it was the development of maritime links with West Africa which led to the growth of a sizeable Black population. By the time the early British colonies had gained a foothold in the Caribbean and the North America, economic ties had been created via the 'triangular trade'. As the slave industry developed more Blacks came to England, some direct from Africa and others via the New World. Many were resold or bartered in England through advertisements in London (Walvin 1992).

According to the "Gentleman's Magazine", there were 20,000 Black people in London in 1764 (Walvin 1984: 33-34). Most of them were poor. Some, such as Francis Barber and Olaudah Equiano, rose to fame, whilst others like Billy Water, the one legged fiddler dubbed the 'King of Beggars', gained notoriety. The treatment of Blacks in the late eighteenth and early nineteenth century ranged from brutality to friendship and intimacy. Blacks in London formed their own social and political groups to campaign for the liberation of Black slaves and to offer them assistance and security (Fraser 1984).

Early contact with Africans set the stage for the racial attitudes which have permeated society in Britain to the present day. As Walvin (1984: 32) explains:

Europeans had long known of the more exotic people from distant parts of the world ... of the bizarre and strange sights of human nature to be found lurking beyond the pale of European society ... Few offered a more startling contrast to contemporary values of beauty, social virtue and godliness than the black Africans.

The racism clearly evidenced throughout the eighteenth century was used to keep Black people in their place. Britain's economic power, for instance, was dependent on slavery and the attitudes which sustained the oppression of Black people (Fryer 1984).

By the nineteenth century, the Black population had declined. A few slaves returned to Sierra Leone in 1787. They were also shipped to the Caribbean because of the successful campaign against the slave trade in 1807 (mainly brought about by Black slaves) and the decline in Britain's interest in the West Indies, which coincided with expansion to other parts of the globe and the advent of the Industrial Revolution.

Even though the Black population decreased, it continued to make a mark on British society. Notable Black people included William Curray, the radical Chartist, Ira Aldridge, the famous actor, and Mary Seacole, the nurse who tended to the wounds of British soldiers in the Crimean War. Africans also arrived throughout the nineteenth century as students, runaway slaves or sailors. Black sailors, however, were by far the largest group. They established their roots in British maritime communities such as Cardiff and Liverpool. Blacks also served in the army during the First World War (cf Fryer 1984).

In the early twentieth century Black people were exposed to open discrimination in all aspects of life including the Trade Union Movement. Blacks were criticised for taking work from local Whites and also for having sexual relationships with White women - a theme which preoccupied contemporary society (Walvin 1984). By 1921, the repatriation of Black people was being widely advocated and, within a short period of time, racial hatred was spilling over into riots in Cardiff, Liverpool and London. Continuing discrimination led ultimately to the foundation of the League of Coloured People by the Jamaican, Harold Moody, in 1931.

The anti-imperialistic Pan-African movement emerged in the inter-war years. Black publications, for example, *West Africa* and *The Keys* grew in popularity. Other organisations and journals concerned with Black problems and Black freedom in Africa and the Caribbean were also established (Walvin 1984). They found political allies in many British left-wing groups. The Italian invasion of Ethiopia also had an effect on Black nationalism in Britain.

During the early years of the Second World War, Black workers were incorporated into the workforce. Britain also opened its doors to a number of different nationalities, including their European neighbours and American soldiers, many of whom were Black. There is evidence that Caribbean troops were subjected to similar forms of racial discrimination as those experienced by African-American soldiers in the American army (James 1980).

Post-War Migration

Immediately after the war, many Black soldiers were shipped back to their respective islands. However, some remained and were joined by increasing numbers of Caribbean people who came to Britain to fill the labour gap in the post-war period. In 1951 there were some 15,000 Caribbean newcomers. America had been the traditional destination for Caribbean people but their entry as restricted because of new legislation, most notably the 1952 McCarren-Warren Act. Therefore, Britain became the natural focus for migration.

The early migrants came from islands that had historic links with Britain such as Jamaica, Barbados, Montserrat and St Kitts. In some cases British organisations like London Transport and regional hospital boards launched recruiting drives in the Caribbean (Walvin 1984). Many Jamaicans, in particular, were recruited, through a network of travel agents. In Barbados, the authorities provided loans and assistance for local migrants.

The extent of population movement varied enormously from island to island. In 1960, for example, 9.2 per cent of Jamaican population and 31.5 per cent of Montserratians emigrated to the United Kingdom, but less than 2 per cent of Trinidadians and Tobagans. The figures below ere compiled by the Migrant Services Division of the West Indian Federation Office and place the total number of Caribbeans entering the United Kingdom in 1961 at 238,000.

Emigrants as percentage of West Indian Populations

	Population from 1960 Census	Total emigration to UK 1955-61	Emigrants as % of population
Jamaica	1,609,814	148,369	9.2
Barbados	232,085	18,741	8.1

Trin & Tobago	825,700	9,610	1.2
British Guiana	558,769	7,141	1.3
Leewards	122,920	16,025	13.0
Antigua	54,060	4,687	8.7
Montserrat	12,167	3,835	31.5
St Kitts-Nevis	56,693	7,503	13.2
-Anguilla			
Windwards	314,995	27,154	8.6
Dominica	59,479	7,915	13.3
Grenada	88,617	7,663	8.6
St Lucia	86,194	7,291	8.5
St Vincent	80,705	4,285	5.3

Source: Peach (1968:15)

According to Brown (1985: 61) approximately half of the Caribbean population live in Greater London; 15 per cent in the West Midlands; 2 per cent in the East Midlands and 9 per cent in the North. Caribbean people are thus concentrated in a relatively small number of areas of the country.

Most early immigrants were young men without dependants (Foner 1979). Later migrants were mainly women and children. Dodgson (1865:64) captures some of the experiences of Caribbean women who migrated to Britain during this time:

> Life was much harder for women than it was for men... I used to have to take the two children to the child-minder and go to work in the factory - I had to catch the bus at half-past five ... I come back and use the coal fire. They rent you a room but you can't do anything ... sometimes you had to hide the iron ... You think it is little hardness we suffer in this country?

The 1960s saw the enactment of progressively more stringent legislation and by the 1970s immigration had virtually come to a halt. By 1971 the total Caribbean population in Britain was estimated at 1.5 per cent of the population. Well over a third of the current Black population is British born and over half of those who are immigrants have been in Britain for more than 20 years

(Brown 1985: 17-20). The overall numbers of new immigrants now arriving in Britain is smaller than the numbers returning to the Caribbean.

There has been considerable debate about reasons for migration. the 'push-pull' model, for instance, which distinguishes between the push of economic necessity in the migrant's home society and the pull of work opportunities abroad is often advanced to explain population movement (cf Foner 1979). However, such an approach overlooks the complexity of migration and, as some critics have pointed out, tends to suggest that people are merely reacting to forces beyond their control. Peach (1968), for instance, believes that Caribbean migration did not initially occur during periods of economic depression or high increases in population, but simply in response to a single external stimulus - the demand for labour in Britain. The economic expansion of post-war Britain meant upward mobility for many British workers and the creation of gaps at the lower ends of the occupation ladder. Jamaicans, as well as other Caribbeans, Indians and Pakistanis were drawn in as replacement labour.

Other factors attracted Caribbean immigrants to Britain, too. The Caribbean's colonial past meant there were strong links with Britain. The British system was the model for government and education. As indicated in the discussion of the Caribbean above, British history and English literature dominated the school curriculum. Britain, was projected very much as the mother-land (Hiro 1973).

Responses to Racism
Ever since their arrival, Blacks in Britain have faced racism at every level of society. Disproportionate numbers of Black people are faced with the worst features of urban deprivations: bad housing, low wages and poor education. It is useful at this point to consider each of these areas in turn.

The housing circumstances of Black people in Britain are in many ways inferior to those of Whites. Blacks end to occupy less desirable property, whether it be private or council, than Whites.

Black people tend to be housed because they are homeless whereas Whites are more often allocated property for other reasons. The property occupied by Black tenants is inferior to that occupied by Whites and Blacks tend to wait longer for house transfer than Whites. Black people tend to have lower earnings and therefore less capital invested in property. The areas they live are perceived as posing problems (Brown 1985: 78-94). While there is evidence that the housing conditions of Black people have improved significantly since their initial settlement in Britain, substantial inequalities between Whites and Black remain (HMSO 1991).

Employment is another area of concern. Several studies have been conducted which show widespread discrimination. Both the 1974 PEP survey and the 1992 survey describe in some detail the position that Black workers occupy. Unemployment rates among Black people have been estimated to be twice as high as those for Whites. The average length of unemployment for Black men, especially those who reside outside London, is considerably higher (Brown 1985). It has been calculated that over half of Black unemployed men have been registered for over a year, compared with a third of White unemployed men. Similarly, twice as many Black women as White are unemployed over a long period of time. It should also be noted that an estimated 5 per cent of Black youths under the age of 25 do not view unemployment registration as a realistic way to find work and are not included in official statistics (Brown 1985). The last major survey of this area was undertaken in the early 1980s. There is very little information currently available which throws light on whether there has been any improvement in such trends during the recession of the 1990s. However, a recent study conducted by HMSO (1991) suggests that unemployment rates for Black people, especially men, are still higher than those for the White population.

It is widely assumed that the disparity between Black and White job levels is less pronounced among men and women with qualifications than among those without. However, Troyna & Smith (1983) suggest that higher academic qualifications do not guarantee success among black people in the employment market.

The fact that qualifications do not ensure parity is, he argues, particularly de-motivating.

Educational Underachievement
The situation in education is scarcely less depressing. The inability or unwillingness of the British school system to help Black children fulfil their academic potential has been extensively discussed (Stone 1981; Milner 1983; Tomlinson 1984; Yekwai 1988). The early arrival of Black children in British schools was fraught with difficulties. There was some confusion. for instance, concerning their language needs, especially as parents insisted that their children spoke English while teachers experienced difficulty in understanding them. Concern about Black children and their performance in school was voiced as early as the 1950s. In 1963, a study by Brent LEA found the performance of African-Caribbean children was, on average, lower than whites in reading, arithmetic and spelling. Throughout this period, children were often placed in low streams and remedial classes or in 'special' schools (Townsend 1971). The over-representation of Black children in schools for the educationally sub-normal became a very emotive issue in the early seventies (Coard 1971), for instance, eloquently describes the anger of the Black community about the educational performance of their children.

While awareness of underachievement grew throughout the 1970s, there was little evidence that attempts to address this issue were effective. The Rampton Report (1981), confirmed that Black children were making little progress in the education system, although there were some indications that Black girls performed better than boys (Driver 1980). The Swan Report (1985) also points to widespread underachievement. The picture of achievement which emerges from recent research is highly complex. It would seem that second generation Black pupils tend to achieve higher than the first (Maugham & Rutter 1986). There is also evidence that, while African-Caribbean tend to underperform as a group, there are important within group differences associated with gender and socio-economic groups (Drew & Grey 1990). Underperformance would not appear, however, to be associated with low aspirations: African-Caribbean extend their education beyond school leaving age by approximately three years (Eggleston et al 1986).

The most common theory put forward to explain the underperformance of Black children in the early years of migration was that they were experiencing 'culture shock'. As was the case in America, it was later argued that one of the consequences for Black children living in a racist society was a poor self-esteem (Little 1975) which in turn, results in poor academic achievement. The educational philosophy of multi-cultural education which gained prominence in the 1980s was based on the view that children would perceive themselves more positively and thus achieve better academically if schools acknowledged and respected minority languages and cultures. This position has, however, been widely criticised by writers who point to its inadequacy in reversing observed trends to educational underperformance in Black children (cf Massey 1991). They argue that the need to focus instead on the various manifestations of 'institutional racism' (cf The Rampton Report 1981) which deny Black children access to equality of opportunity in education.

Multiculturalism has given way to anti-racist education as the most persuasive explanation for educational underperformance. One aspect of this institutional racism is teacher attitudes. Mabey (1981), for instance, draws attention to teacher perceptions that African-Caribbean pupils are more likely to come from less culturally stimulating environments and to have parents who are not as interested in their child's education as their White peers. Such negative perceptions can work against children in two ways: firstly they may be internalised by Black children who behave in accordance with the stereotypes secondly, such negative perceptions deny children access to particular groupings or activities.

In a study of Inner London junior school children, Mortimore et al (1988), for instance, show that a significant number of Black pupils who scored highly on tests at the primary level were misplaced in lower bands on entering he secondary school. The study highlighted the 'school process' which suggests that racist practices, such as inappropriate placement within bands, may well be a cause for underachievement.

Different World View

The responses of Black people to the systematic inequalities or oppression which confront them have been various. It is important to remember, that British Blacks by no means form a homogeneous community. Factors which need to be considered include whether or not the individual in question was born in Britain or came originally from the Caribbean. The age at which they came is also crucial, for there are differences in the expectations of adult and child migrants. Differences in personality and individual experiences also have to be taken into account, as they exert an important influence on response to life in Britain.

Various writers have suggested typologies of British Black society. Pryce (1979), for instance, identifies six different groups: hustlers, teenyboppers, proletarian, respectable, saints, mainliners and in-betweeners. Troyna (1979) looks at Black youth in terms of mainstreamers, compromisers and rejecters. Henry et al (1982) give a typology of African-Caribbean identities which includes West Indians, colonial settlers, civil rights Blacks, Black nationalists and Pan Africanists. Categorisations of this kind of the Black community may, however, be over simplistic and misleading. Pryce (1979), for instance, gives group status to the relatively small numbers engaged in criminal activity and thus reinforces stereotypes of Black people (Figueroa 1982). By the same token, such categories are often meaningless to the Black community. None the less, classification of this kind provides a useful starting point for the discussion of a complex phenomenon which can probably best be described in terms of a continuum of attitudes and behaviours. For the purposes of the present discussion, attention will be focused on two groups, universally acknowledged as distinct within the British Black community, which lie at polar ends of the continuum: Rastafarians and Christians.

Rastafarianism

The Rastafari movement has its origins in Jamaica in the 1930s. Its ideology of Black consciousness and Pan-Africanism began with Marcus Garvey, who urged Jamaicans to return to Africa. The origins and growth of the Rastafarian movement need to be seen against the background of the social conditions of colonial Jamaica, which led some of the rural poor to reject British rule and identify instead with the Ethiopian monarch, Haile Selassie, or Ras Tafari, whom they considered the living God who would use his power to help Black people to return to the fatherland, Africa. When this prophecy was not fulfilled, there was a gradual shift of focus from the return to African to Jamaican liberation (Barrett 1977).

Reggae music, popularised by artists such as Bob Marley and Jimmy Cliff, is the vehicle for Rastafari songs of defiance and inspiration and offers social commentary on the collective experience or racism. Rastas have also adapted the Jamaican language to mould their own distinctive style of speech, known as Rasta talk. 'Oversand' for undersand and 'I an I' for we are just some examples of their creative use of language.

Rastafarianism was viewed with much suspicion in Britain, until it gained greater recognition by political leaders like Michael Manley in Jamaica in the 1960s and 1970s, and early migrants still remember it as a somewhat disreputable cult. They feel their British offspring are merely following the fashion. However, the attraction of an alliterative life style and values which affirm Black culture for young people seriously disillusioned with the treatment they have received in Britain should not be underestimated. Interestingly, in many parts of Britain, Rastafarianism seems to be declining in popularity and the Black muslim religion, developed in America, is beginning to attract many young people, especially in London, no doubt for reasons similar to those which brought Rastafarianism to prominence in the 1970s.

Black British Pentecostalism

Black Pentecostalism which has already been discussed in relation to the Caribbean, is a rather different response to the realities of life in Britain. It is a major religious movement which has received relatively little academic attention. The work of Hill (1963), Calley (1965), MacRoberts (1989) Edwards (1992) and Gerloff (1992), however, provide some insight into Black British Pentecostalism.

It has been estimated some 69 per cent of the migrants who came to Britain in the fifties and sixties were regular church goers. The shock and confusion experienced by the early migrants upon discovering that England was not the promised land of Christianity receives some attention from Hill (1963). The difficulties that the early migrants experienced in local White churches, however, have only recently been documented. Anecdotal evidence drawn from Caribbean migrants suggests that they felt excluded by their fellow Christians. Much White racism was unintentional (Sutcliffe and Tomlin 1986: 16-7), although there have been some case of Black Christians being told by White ministers not to revisit their Churches. Racism was certainly an important factor in the emergence of Black churches (Brooks 1982).

Cross-cultural misunderstanding may also have played a role in Black people's disappointment with White Christianity, traditional reserve being interpreted as hostility. There were cross-generational considerations, too. Most migrants in the 1950s were young, whereas the congregations in White inner city churches were often elderly. As MacRoberts (1989: 128) explains:

> The black Pentecostal congregation was - and still is a haven of 'warmth', 'life' and cultural familiarity in the midst of a white Christianity which the first generation often perceived as unloving, powerless and paternalistic.

The problems which Caribbean people experienced in meeting their spiritual needs in Britain inevitably led to the growth of Black Pentecostal churches. It is estimated that there are some 650

Black Pentecostal churches with 40,000 members. The largest, New Testament Church of God, for example, has approximately one hundred churches and a membership of 8,000 people. Black churches are not just the stronghold of first generation Caribbean people. They continue to attract young British born people, though females greatly outnumber males.

As already indicated, the style of worship of many Blacks in America, Jamaica and later in Britain represents a remodelling of Christianity within an African cultural framework. Black Pentecostal worship is both collective and expressive. Edwards (1992: 68) describes the pattern of worship as 'organised spontaneity'.

Some writers have described the growth of Pentecostalism as a buffer for the harsh realities of the outside world (Cashmore 1979). In spite of the conservative nature of their worship, Black Pentecostal Christians have been active in self-help organisations and there has been a move towards involvement with social and political issues (Arnold 1992). This has been expressed through discussion and debate in organisations such as the African-Caribbean alliance which has been established with the aim of unifying Black churches.

Conclusion
African people were enslaved and brought to the Caribbean, America and Britain at the beginning of the sixteenth century. Slavery, the institution, responsible for the destination of Africans in the New World lasted for over four hundred years and has had an enormous impact on Black people in the Diaspora. There were very similar social and economic conditions in America and the Caribbean. Britain was implicated in this, but at a distance. In both the Caribbean and America, Blacks worked mainly in the sugar and cotton plantation fields. Through the system of slavery they have all experienced brutality and human degradation.

A comparison of the history of Black people in the Caribbean and North America thus shows many important parallels. In both cases, society has been shaped by European colonisation; in both cases slavery has moulded the political, social and economic life and expectations of both Black and White people; in both cases, Blacks have strongly resisted the forces of White oppression over the centuries. We have gradually arrived at a situation where Black people have considerably more power and wealth outside Africa, than at any point in the last 300 years, but the legacy of colonialism has ensured that most Black people still remain at the bottom of the social and economic ladder and an underclass has emerged.

There are important differences in the experiences of Black people in the Diaspora which date back to the days of slavery. In the Caribbean, Africans formed the majority. Significantly, in the post-independence period, they have managed to increase their influence in government and other institutions. However, large proportions of the population remain in poverty and have limited educational opportunities. While the legacy of colonial rule is still to be felt, all Caribbean states are now mainly controlled by politicians of African heritage.

In contrast, in America Black people are in the minority. Nonetheless, their situation is remarkably similar to that of African-Caribbeans. Until the 1960s they experienced racial segregation, particularly in the south where the Jim Crow Laws were legally enforced. While there has been some improvement, as witnessed, for example, by the development of a Black middle class, the majority find themselves as seriously disadvantaged as they were earlier in the century.

The Black British experience is perhaps closer to that of Blacks in America than those in the Caribbean. In Britain, Blacks also form a minority. Despite the fact, that there has been a Black presence since Elizabethan times, significant numbers of settlers from the Caribbean only began arriving in the post-war period. Since that time, they have been subjected to the same kinds of oppression experienced by African-Americans and there is widespread evidence of racism in the areas of employment, housing and education.

The ways in which Black people have experienced oppression has given rise to a culture of resistance. Despite what some White historians have suggested, Blacks have always resisted Whites, resulting in African cultural retentions in religions, language and other aspects of African culture. The common experiences of oppression explains the cultural and linguistics similarities that form the focus for the chapters which follow and make it possible for us to talk in terms of 'Black speech' and 'Black culture'.

CHAPTER 3

BLACK LANGUAGE

∞ ∞ ∞

In previous chapter, the focus was on the history of the African Diaspora in the Caribbean, America and Britain. In this chapter, we turn to the exploration of the language of these groups, drawing attention to the extensive similarities between structures of geographically dispersed varieties of Black language and examining the historical events which led to their development. Particular emphasis is placed on attitudes towards Black language on the part of both minority and majority group speakers, and on the roles which these have played both in maintaining the distinctiveness of Black speech and in ensuring the continued educational under performance of Black children.

The origins of Black language in the Caribbean, America and Britain can be traced directly to West Africa. West African languages belong to the Niger-Kordofanian family which can be divided into the following main branches (Dalphinis 1991: 33).

NIGER-KORDOFANIAN

MANDE WEST ADAMAWA GUR KRU KWA BENUE KORDOFANIAN
       ATLANTIC EASTERN   -CONGO

Bambara Wolof Sango Mossi Efik Yoruba Swahili Koalib
(Mandinka) Pula

                           Ibo   Lingala
                           Ewe   Kikongo
                           Akan

FIGURE 3.1 The Niger-Kordofanian language family

In spite of the variety of West African languages, the close structural inter-relationships between them were observed as early as 1700 by writers such as Labat (1728 cited in Dalphinis 1991: 34) and, more recently, by scholars such as Dalphinis (1991 and Dillard (1972). As Dalphinis (1991 34) puts it.

> Their structural similarities, in contrast with their dissimilarities in vocabulary, point to ways of classifying language/dialect differences other than those based on differences in sounds and vocabulary, which are more dominant as traditions in distinguishing between European languages ... The differences in the languages concerned are often those of vocabulary rather than structure.

During the Atlantic slave trade, there was a deliberate policy of separating Africans who spoke the same language(s) as a means of ensuring maximum control and preventing rebellion (Herskovits 1958). Contact with Europeans was limited and it would seem that those Africans who interacted with White slavers and overseers spoke good, easily intelligible English. The main challenge for the African majority was thus to develop a means of communication between themselves.

The Development of Pidgins and Creoles
In order to understand the development of Black speech in the Americas it is helpful to discuss pidgins and creoles and the theories concerning their origin. A pidgin is a marginal language fulfilling restricted communication needs (De Camp 1971a; Romaine 1988). The process of pidginization is characterised by reduction: lexical items are restricted to the bare minimum and syntax is greatly simplified. Over subsequent generations, however, the pidgin gradually becomes the mother tongue of a speech community. A process of expansion and elaboration leads to the development of a creole which can be considered as a full language in its own right. As Todd (1974: 3):

A creole arises when a pidgin becomes the other tongue of a speech community. The simple structure that characterised the pidgin is carried over into the creole but since a creole, as a mother tongue, must be capable of expressing the whole range of human experience, the lexicon is expanded and frequently a more elaborate syntactic system evolves.

There has been a great deal of debate around the origins of pidgins and creoles (cf Todd 1974; Romaine 1988). The baby talk theory for instance, maintains that pidgins and creoles have resulted from the inadequate attempts of African and Asiatic speakers to gain control of European languages (Bloomfield 1933: 472-3). A second theory takes the view that a nautical jargon used on ships for communication among sailors of different nationalities was passed on to Africans, Asians and others (cf Matthews 1935). Neither the baby talk theory nor the nautical jargon theory, however, can account for the astonishing similarities between pidgins and creoles across time and space. One reaction to this has been the monogenetic theory of origins which is based on the notion that all pidgins are genetically related to one proto-pidgin, a relexified version of a fifteenth-century Portuguese pidgin, the medieval lingua franca Sabir, which was first used along the African coast and later carried to Asia. Alternative explanations for the similarities, however, have also been advanced. The polygenetic or independent parallel theory of origins, for instance, was first postulated by Hall (1961). The essence of this theory is that pidgins and creoles arose independently but developed in parallel.

Of particular importance for the discussion of the Black language of the Diaspora, however, is the African substratum theory which draws attention to the various African linguistic features, (including phonological, syntactic and lexical) that can be found in many pidgins and creoles. There is certainly widespread evidence to support this position. Goodman (1964), for example, argues that only the West African origin of all French creoles can explain their similarities. Alleyne (1980) attributes African-American dialects to a common set of structural features among West African languages which persists in the New World.

Sutcliffe (1992) also provides African-based explanations for Caribbean creoles and African-American varieties. Since many of the slaves came from multilingual communities which share African grammatical structures, it is argued that the languages which developed are adaptations based on African rules.

It should be remembered, however, that while the evidence of African influence is extremely persuasive, other factors also need to be taken into consideration. Many of the features found in the Black languages of the diaspora are also to be found in creoles where there has been no contact with African languages. For example, pidgins and creoles which belong to the Pacific area have similarities with African-based ones, such as second person plural pronouns and a limited number of gender distinctions (cf Todd 1974: 15-17).

Largely in response to observations of this kind, Bickerton (1984) has attempted to explain the origins of creoles in terms of a universal human biogram for language. His views are largely based on a comparison of evidence from creole grammars and studies of child language acquisition. He claims that the incorrect structures which characterise children's language acquisition are similar to those evident in creole grammars. The features children learn naturally are the ones which the children of first generation creole speakers learn in the absence of direct input from the speech of others in the community. However, Bickerton's claims are contentious. Although language acquisition is a creative and on-going process, it would seem that children do not create their own language but rather follow one that is already in existence, which they reproduce and transform (cf Romaine 1988: 275).

While the debate around the linguistic processes which gave rise to pidgins and creoles continues unabated, it is none the less possible to build a picture of the historical conditions surrounding their development in the Caribbean and America before their transfer to Britain. Let us look first at the linguistic situation in the Caribbean with particular reference to Jamaica.

The Development of Caribbean Creoles

The linguistic history of the Caribbean is extremely complex. The Spanish, Portuguese, Dutch, French and English converged on West Africa in the course of the 15th Century and were implicated in the development of the slave trade. Africans thus found themselves in a situation where they had to communicate not only with other Africans from various areas, but also with Europeans. The situation varied from one island to the next but in Jamaica, for instance, some 9,000 indentured servants came from all over England, speaking their own dialects, while Cromwell shipped a large Irish population (O'Callaghan 1981)). There was also a small French speaking population and later, in the eighteenth century, a significant Scots community came to work as shop-keepers and traders.

By far the largest group, however, were the Africans. The precise origins of West African slaves and their languages are difficult to ascertain, for shipping company accounts are unreliable. However, there is evidence to suggest that the most important areas for the supply of slaves were the Gold Coast where Twi, Ewe and Yoruba were widely spoken, and the Gambia, Sierra Leone and Ivory Coast region where the main mother tongues were Malinke, Banbara, Gola and Kru. In addition, the Papams from the Slave Coast spoke Ewe; and the Ibos from Benin and the Niger Delta spoke a mixture of Hausa, Effik, Yoruba, Ibo and other languages which belong to the Bantu family. This situation gave rise to what some writers (Alleyne 1980) have labelled a proto-pidgin which later developed into a creole.

In a Caribbean context, it seems probably the creole gradually stabilised and became the accepted lingua franca island among slaves, Caribbean-born Whites and the growing mixed race community. Many features of the creole were also to be fond in the speech of native Whites. The degree of language contact was determined by socio-cultural forces. With reference to development of Jamaican Creole (JC) Callaghan (1981) argues that English was the prestige language used by colonial administrators, masters and missionaries but the majority of slaves had little contact with it so that African linguistic and cultural elements were retained, mixed and adapted

During and after slavery the plantation was self-contained both physically and linguistically so that creole had time to stabilise and also remained intact because of the lack of resources, or, no doubt, the lack of will on the part of the colonial policy makers, to impose standard English through formal education. Social, political and economic changes in the twentieth century have brought further linguistic changes in Jamaican and other Caribbean creoles.

Variation in JC

A particularly important feature of language use in the Caribbean is the extent of variation which exists. This variation is often described in terms of a continuum between broad creole (or the basilect) and standard Jamaican English (or the acrolect) (cf Bickerton 1980). For the purpose of illustration, it is helpful to look at the main features at both ends of this continuum and also at the nature of variation.

Sutcliffe (1982: 129), for instance, gives various extracts from the speech of Patrica which illustrate the range of her linguistic repertoire. Take the following examples of narrative:

> This woman she was in her bed... the husband had died ... it was the husband that wasmm ... doin' all the killin' ... he had died long time ago and he had 'is Egyptian ring on (...) a curse was on i dat who die wi' this ring will live again, and the only way you can break that curse is to take the ring off ... well mm ... di girl hear this man bang ... you know crash of glass ... she go outside into (th) is summerhouse and take di gun ... and after the husband 'd died she never gone in there again ... so ... and no window was broken (...) di door ... di lock was forced ... not wid any kin' a weapon ... it ws just like it was turned or some'ing like that ... well she went in there we' di gun and di dog an a torch ...

Note, for instance, that while much of this corresponds closely to standard English, there are also various feature of JC phonology. For example, the use of dental stops for fricatives in di and dat; the deletion of the final consonant in kin', and also JC grammar, hear for heard, go for went and take for took.

... try to open dis box and 'i white boy cut imsel' ... den after suddenly di boy was (...) bandaged an doin' it up fi 'im an suddenly dis ting dis op...'im dis go so like ... im open i...dis kin' a box ... coffin an ma...'im close...'e mouth den a 'im... 'im stan 'up so an get out di grave ... I man 'i coffin, an den after 'e open 'e mout' an 'e walkin down like 'at ...an go-in aaah! showin 'e teet'...an di blood dis drippin' down di mout in it? (...) an 'en after 'e jus' take di bwoy ban' an jus' gone suck out di blood.

Whereas in the first passage JC features like dental stops were used some of the time in the second passage this feature is invariant. Similarly, while the first passage showed variation between inflected and uninflected past tense, the second passage makes no use of inflection to mark past tense except in the case of was.

It is not difficult to see why variation of this kind should be described in terms of a continuum. Some writers (De Camp, 1971b) have gone further to describe the variation which occurs in present-day Jamaica as a post-creole continuum. It is argued that the media and education which have had an important role in the propagation of English have narrowed the gap between basilect (pure creole) and acrolect (Jamaican Standard English).

De Camp (1971b) proposes that in order for this to occur the target language must be the same as the creole vocabulary base. In addition, there has to be sufficient social mobility to motivate a large proportion of creole speakers to modify their speech so that it is closer to the standard and there must be sufficient educational programmes and other acculturative forces for the standard language to exert an influence on the creole. As corrective measures do not have the same effect on all speakers, there will inevitably be a large range of variation between individuals as well as within the same speaker in different situations.

Some writers, for example, Lawton (1980); Alleyne (1980), have questioned the concept of the continuum and have preferred to take in terms of code-switching or code-shifting. Alleyne (1980: 80), for instance, explains the situation in the following terms:

> Speakers are located not at points in the continuum, but in zones, the range of the zone corresponding to the range of their ability to manipulate linguistic forms. Each zone contains a repertoire of linguistic material which a speaker chooses from, his particular choice motivated by the sociological and psychological context of the speech situation. This type of linguistic behaviour has been referred to as code-switching.

African-American Language

The historical development of Black English Vernacular (BEV) or Black English (BE), the language used among African-Americans, is similar to that of Caribbean creoles. An important difference between the Caribbean and America, however, is the relative proportion of African and Europeans. Although there is evidence that Blacks grew to form the majority in some southern states (Foner 1976), it was generally the case that Whites outnumbered Blacks. The relative distribution of these various groups may well have had important implications for the linguistic situation which developed in the different contexts.

Evidence suggests that a West African form of pidgin English was in use in the slave community in the colonies and early days in America as well as in the Caribbean (Dillard 1992). The population of American plantations and ports included many lower class Whites who were mainly from Britain, or in the case of the lower Mississippi area, from France. A number of Blacks brought knowledge of pidgins and creoles with them either from islands such as Barbados or directly from West Africa. There is also evidence that slaves were in close contact with native Americans, especially in the seventeenth and eighteenth centuries.

It is highly probable that a maritime pidgin spoken by the native Americans on the East Coast was transmitted from the native Americans to the slaves (Dillard 1992).

As we saw in Chapter two, the majority of African slaves were concentrated in the south. However, there was also a Black presence in the north and documentary evidence suggests that, in the middle of the eighteenth century, a distinctive variety of English was spoken by at least some of the African heritage residents of New York and Philadelphia. But while some pidgin-like features and African phonology and lexis have been reported in states as far north as Massachusetts, it is likely that a creole either failed to develop or underwent a process of decreolization well before Emancipation. As Dillard (1992: 73) points out:

It took place at different rates among different populations, and complete creolization may never have taken place in some areas where identifiable Black usage can still be traced historically. At least there is evidence of the development of non-creole grammatical forms more nearly resembling on the surface the usage of mainstream Whites but not identical with that usage.

The language found among the Blacks in the Sea Islands of Georgia and South Carolina, known as Gullah Creole or Geechee speech, has particular importance for any discussion of Black language in North America. The Gullah people who form a distinct African-American community have retained considerable West African cultural and language patterns (cf Turner 1949). Gullah speech is significant as BEV may once have had similar features.

A comparison of key features of Caribbean creoles and BEV (see fig 3.2 below) shows that the process of decreolization was far more rapid in the American context.

	JC	BEV
Third pers. sg. pres. tense	+	+

Winstan waak faas (JC)
Winston walk fas' (BEV)

Plurals   +   +
Chrii pliet (JC)
Three plate/three plates (BEV)
Di pakit-dem (JC)
Dem pockets (BEV)
Dem waan dat yeside (JC)
Dey want dat yesterday/ (BEV)
Dey wanted dat yesterday (BEV)

Simple past tense   +   +
Di toun go ssss (JC)
The stone say ssss (BEV)
Dem waan dat yeside (JC)
Dey want dat yesterday (BEV)
Dey wanted dat yesterday(BEV)

First pers. sing. pronoun   +   -
Mi gud (JC)
Am good (BEV)
Mi rait (JC)
Is Am right? (BEV)
A waak de (JC)
A walk there (BEV)
Third pers. sing. pronouns   +   -
Im taiad (JC)
He tired (BEV)
She tired (BEV)

Third pers. pl pronoun   +   +
Dem fiesi (JC)
Dey facety

Negatives   +   +
Winstan no waak faas (JC)
Winston dont walk fas' H/Pr (BEV)
Winston aint walk fas' past (BEV)
Winstan no chuupit (JC)
Winston aint stupid (BEV)

Copula   +   +
W. sista-dem fiesi (JC)
Winston sisters be facety H/P (BEV)
Winston sisters facety (BEV)
Hou dem tan? (JC)
How dey is? (BEV)
Aspect Particles   +   +
Mi a waak (JC)
Am walkin/I'm walking (BEV)
Mi wi waak (JC)
Am a walk - future (BEV)
Mi don waak (JC)
A done walk/I've finished (BEV)
Winstan fiesi (JC)
Winston facety (BEV)
Winston be facety (BEV)
Winstan dide laaf (JC)
Winston steady laughin (BEV)
Demde piich depan raip (JC)
Dem peaches steady be gettin ripe (BEV)

Focus   +   -
A waak yu waak ar a ron yu ron? (JC)
Is you walk or run? (BEV)
A dat yu waan (JC)
Das what you want (BEV)
A no ron Winstan ron! (JC)
Winston <u>run!</u>

Questions   +   +
She tel Winstan? (JC)
She tell Winston? (BEV)
Is she tell Winston? (BEV)
A wa mek yu kyaan dwiit? (JC)
What make you caint do it? (BEV)
A huu dat? (JC)
Who dat? (BEV)

Infinitives   +   -
Winstan waan se/Winstan waan fi se (JC)
Winston want say/ Winston wanta say (BEV)
Winstan go de fi tel dem (JC)
Winston went there to gon tell dem (BEV)

Other Pronouns   +   +
Unu fi dwiit (JC)
Y'all gotta do it (BEV)
Who-all ... ? (BEV)
Das a gud wan (JC)
Das* a good one (BEV)

Psychic state   +   +
Winstan tingk se ... (JC)
Winston think da ... (BEV)
Ted dat man se yu shiem (JC)
Tell da man say you sorry (BEV)

'Dem' Plurals   +   +
Winstan-dem (JC)
Winston n em (BEV)
Winston-dem (rare conservative) (BEV)
Di pliet-dem (JC)
Dem plates (BEV)

Locating verbs   +   -
Winstan pen de pan di tiebl (JC)
Winston pen is on the table (BEV)
Winston pen on the table (BEV)

* In both JC and BEV, <u>das</u> can be considered a pronoun it its own right (and <u>not</u> a contraction). The same is true of <u>Am.</u>

Equating verbs   +   -
Mi bes fren a mi woman (JC)
Ma bes friend is ma woman/ma bes friend ma woman (BEV)
Mi bes fren woz mi woman (JC)

Ma bes friend was* ma woman (BEV)
Marjory bes fren no Jenny *** (JC)
Marjory bes friend aint Jenny (BEV)
Im go ton tiicha (JC)
She gon be a teacher (BEV)
A two gyal ina di ruum (JC)
Iss two gals in tfhe room (BEV)
* Pronounced <u>wuz</u> rhyming with <u>does</u>
*** Sometimes <u>no</u> is used - eg, M. bes fren no Jenny

Past marker   +   +
Winstan bena waak (JC)
Winston been walkin (BEV)
Marjory ben nuo dat (laangtaim) (JC)
Marjory been know that (stressed been remote past) (BEV)
Im no en anastan dat (JC)
He aint understand dat (BEV)
Dadi woz taiad (JC)
Daddy was* tired
* Pronounced <u>wuz</u> rhyming with <u>does</u>

The Divergence Hypothesis
The more rapid rate of decreolization in North America can no
doubt be explained in terms of the larger ratio of Africans to
Europeans in the Caribbean; it may also be related to the greater
level of social mobility in America, where a significant middle
class community has evolved. Even within America, there is
considerable disagreement as to whether Black English is
currently diverging from or converging towards standard English
(SE). Smitherman (1977: 11) discusses this phenomenon in the
following terms:

The "push-pull" momentum is evidenced in the historical
development of Black English in the push toward Americanization
of Black English counterbalanced by the pull of retaining its
Africanization. We may use the term 'de-creolization' to refer to
the push toward Americanizing of the language. As slaves became
more American and less African, the Black English Creole also
became less Africanized.

Predictions in the 1960s and 1970s that the impact of racial integration, the media and increased educational opportunities would result in the de-creolization of Black speech, have not, according to the divergence argument, been fulfilled. Dayton's (1981, 1983) long term study of tense and aspect in the Philadelphia Black community, for instance, provides evidence that BEV is becoming more remote from SE. Bailey and Maynor (1985a) also support this position, as do Labov & Harris (1986: 2), who point to the role of racial segregation in maintaining linguistic difference. In their view:

There is a close parallel between residential segregation and linguistic segregation, and between residential segregation and educational failure.

They argue that Blacks in Philadelphia, where their study was based, use a form of English which is different from that of Whites and that the differences appear to be increasing. Labov & Harris believe that their study reflects a national trend in the Black community toward linguistic divergence. Whereas linguistic features passed freely between different ethnic groups, such as the Italians and Greeks in the White community, the same features were not shared between Black and White speakers. Black speakers appeared to use a form of BEV that was very similar to that studied in New York, Los Angeles and many other areas. They cite distinct grammatical features of BEV such as the absence of subject-verb agreement as evidence for this. Significantly, the degree to which such features were exhibited depended on a whole range of factors which included the degree to which the individual interacted with white people.

Labov & Harris (1986) also point out that linguistic segregation is not just a matter of race but also of class. In earlier periods of African-American history, working class Black youths were in close contact with middle class peers who had considerable command of the standard. Now, however, many middle class Blacks have moved out of the inner city.

Ash & Myhill (1986) also show that blacks who come into close contact with whites go a long way towards acquiring white speech patterns, but whites who mix with Blacks made very little progress towards acquiring the Black patterns. This suggests that the factors of central importance to this problem are prestige and the need of speakers to maintain solidarity with the Black community.

The Convergence Hypothesis

Other studies offer a rather different analysis of the features provided as evidence for divergence and subscribe to the view that BEV is converging on the standard. Supporters of this position argue that the effects of education are leading the English spoken by African-Americans to converge on Standard English. Nichols (1986 cited in Vaughn-Cooke 1987)), for instance, investigated the use of prepositions and pronouns by Blacks in George Town County, South Carolina. and found that speakers are moving toward a regional Standard English. Similarly Bailey & Bassett (1986) studied invariant BE in the speech patterns of Blacks in three areas in the South - East Louisiana, Gulf Mississippi and Lower Mississippi. Their data point to fewer young speakers using non-standard features. They claim that, while Blacks of all ages use invariant BE, it is most common in the speech of older people, with 79 per cent of informants over the age of 65 but only 40 per cent of those under 65 using the feature.

Vaughn-Cooke's (1986 cited in Vaughn-Cooke 1987) cross-generational study of 40 black working class people in the Mississippi area is also significant. She investigates variations in the pronunciation of words containing unstressed syllables (for example *afraid, across, electric, America*) that represent a phonological change in progress. All speakers pronounced words like *afraid* and *electric* both with and without the initial syllable. Her study supports the view that Black English is converging rather than diverging from the standard.

Vaughn-Cooke (1987) is highly critical of the divergence hypothesis on the grounds that its exponents do not give a sufficiently detailed analysis of how the language has changed. In her view insufficient attention is given, for example, to age. Thus she argues that the invariant BE cited by Bailey & Maynor (1985a) as representing language change provides evidence instead for age-grading. Wolfram (1987) and Spears (1987) also reject the divergence hypothesis because the generational differences needed to substantiate the claim have not been presented.

In trying to reconcile the viewpoints of convergence and divergence theorists, it is important to remember the complexities of the social realities which are responsible for linguistic change. On the one hand, African-Americans have made considerable social gains. As such, one would predict that their speech patterns would rapidly converge on those of mainstream English. As Wilson (1980; 1987) points out, socio-economic factors may well be replacing race as the main determinants of life chances for individual Blacks. However, it would seem that the vast majority of African-Americans have made relatively little progress. Jaynes & Williams (1989) argue, for instance, that Blacks are suspicious of American institutions. They are still segregated in public schools and places of residence and their outlook on life reflects an awareness of their disadvantaged position. As Nash (1991) points out, middle class Blacks who are involved in the mainstream institutions of education may be doing so through the 'lens of non-standard language' and may inadvertently be excluded from some of the effects of participation. He also argues that Black women, in particular, may be excluded from full participation because their loyalty to the mother tongue is very deeply rooted. In this view, then, it is highly probable that Black speech patterns will continue to diverge.

Divergence versus Convergence in Writing
The question of divergence and convergence in written American standard English is equally important for the debate. Smitherman (1992) examines this issue using national samples of 17 year old African-Americans in the National Assessment of Educational Progress (NAEP), from 1969-1979 and 1984-1988/89. Her study seeks to highlight the frequency and distribution of BEV in writing over a generation. Different types of essays, ranging from

narrative to discursive, were analysed. One of the most significant results is that the frequency of BEV in all essays throughout the year groups is generally low. Black English Vernacular speech patterns are only minimally reproduced in writing.

Black English declined in the narrative essays from 1969-1979, but not in the descriptive/discursive essays. In fact, in the 1979 descriptive essays there was an increase in some features of BEV, for example irregular verbs and subject-verb agreement. The copula patterns which indicate the African substratum that characterises Black English were also evident.

Overall, however, comparison of the two sets of data offer clear evidence for convergence. The analysis of BEV in essays by African-American 17 year olds over a generation shows a significant decline in the use of Black English since 1969. The pattern of decline in BEV in the NAEP essays thus raises questions about the validity of the divergence hypothesis - at least in writing - over the past 20 years. As Smitherman (1992: 57) asserts:

This result, in combination with the present study's findings about the decline in Black English production over time, strengthens the case for convergence in the direction of Edited American/Standard English over the past 20 years, at least in writing, if not in speech.

Possible reasons for convergence in writing are diverse. One explanation, is the fact that writers are not penalised for BEV in terms of their accomplishment of specific writing tasks. Linguistic diversity policies and numerous forums, beginning in the 1970s, have raised teachers' awareness of language issues and may well have had an impact on the linguistic freedom of African-American students. Another explanation is that Black students seem to have become more adept in their command of written English, perhaps due to increased exposure to formal education. However, it needs to be remembered that de-creolization is more evident in writing than in speech. In fact, according to Smitherman (1992), the rich verbal and linguistic traditions are diverging and developing new features in American popular culture forms, as can be seen, for example, in the use of BEV in rap music. The increased ability of African-Americans to code switch from Black to standard English, in comparison with their counterparts in the previous generation, could also be a factor that needs to be considered.

Code-Switching

Code-switching, defined as 'the use of more than one language in the cause of a single communicative episode' (Heller 1988) is widespread in multilingual speech communities. There are also indications that it is a more prevalent feature in dialect-speaking communities than has traditionally been assumed. Taylor (1975: 36) surveyed a group of Black adolescents from southern and border states from whom he elicited a 70 per cent response to the question: 'Can you switch dialects easily?' In reporting his findings Taylor (1975: 37) states that:

> Dialect switching is a commonly observed phenomenon, especially among older and better educated Blacks.

DeBose (1992) is critical of previous research which tended to ignore code-switching and focus on the speech patterns of lower-class Blacks. In his view, code-switching, particularly among the middle-class, has not seriously been considered. Dillard (1972), for instance, seems to under-estimate the level of bidialectalism which exists, believing that most middle-class Blacks are monolingual speakers of standard English. Wolfram (1969), in his Detroit study, describes the African-American language situation in terms of a continuum between the idealised polar lects, suggesting a post-creole continuum model. Wolfram's methodology is in fact particularly ill-suited to studies of code-switching. Whereas code-switching takes place among individual speakers in particular conversational episodes, Wolfram relies upon statistical analysis of the frequency of occurrence of selected grammatical variants in data from groups over a wide range of times and locations.

In contrast, DeBose (1992: 165) provides evidence that code-switching is common in the speech of middle class African-Americans. He uses a small group of middle class African-

Americans who speak both standard English and Black English. His analysis shows that they consider SE the appropriate code for use with outsiders or in mainstream settings and BE for in-group use among African-Americans.

The evidence considered is striking counter evidence to the claim that BE is spoken mainly by poor and uneducated persons. We must await the results of future research for a definitive assessment of the prevalence of BE/SE code switching among African-Americans, but my impression as a member of the speech community is that BE is frequently spoken by middle-class persons. That impression is consistent with the fact that many educated, middle-class African-Americans begin their lives in predominantly-black urban ghettos or rural southern communities where BE is the normal medium of everyday communication. The subsequent upward mobility of such persons usually entails becoming bilingual speakers of BE and SE rather than replacement of BE by SE.

Black Language in Britain
The proportion of Black speakers in Britain is considerably lower than in either of the Caribbean or America. The presence of a significant Black community is also more recent, dating back only to the post-war period. The patterns of Black language use in Britain are thus, predictably, rather different from those in the other locations under discussion.

In the years following the main period of settlement in Britain, the number of British born Black-children who could speak a variety of English similar or indistinguishable from the local White norm grew considerably. Some children appeared to be bilingual. Therefore, some interesting questions were raised about patterns of language used among these children. From the perspective of White commentators, the most important feature of the first generation of British born Black children was the apparent ease with which they were linguistically assimilated to the local speech norms. Rosen & Burgess (1980) for instance, report that only 20% of Jamaicans and 10% of the children from Eastern Caribbean territories have Jamaican or other Caribbean creole as their dominant speech or use it regularly in certain contexts; while 80% of Jamaican and 90% children from East Caribbean are basically London or standard speakers who occasionally have creole features.

The ability to speak British English was thus assumed to imply that British Black children were rapidly losing the ability to speak a Black variety. For the purposes of the present study, this distinctively British variety will be termed Patois, following community usage. Several studies, however, have thrown doubt on this interpretation. Sutcliffe (1978; 1982), for example, used a questionnaire in structured group interviews and found that some 88% of the Caribbean born and 79% of the British born were able to speak what he describes as 'broad creole'. Hadi (1976) who used a modified form of the questionnaire in a multiracial comprehensive school in the Midlands obtained similar results. These finding are difficult to reconcile with Rosen and Burgess' (1980) study.

The picture becomes more confusing still when reference is made to Tomlin's (1981) study of a random sample of young people under the age 25 in Dudley in which 100% of respondents admitted to speaking Patois in some situations. Edwards (1983; 1986) suggests that discrepancies of this kind can be largely explained by examining the methodologies employed by these researchers. Rosen and Burgess' figures, for instance, were based on teacher estimates or requests for information from pupils and are likely to have resulted in serious under-reporting (see Nicholas 1994, for a critique of language surveys). Sutcliffe and Hadi, in contrast, established positive attitudes towards Black language before eliciting views from children in group interviews. And the fact that Tomlin is herself a Black researcher is likely to have predisposed respondents to admit to Black speech patterns.

Such surveys, however, beg a number of questions. What does it mean 'to speak Patois'? Are all speakers equally fluent? What are the situations which tend to trigger Black speech patterns? And why do some speakers apparently use more Black features than others? Edwards' (1986) addresses these questions in a study of 45

British born Black adolescents of Jamaican heritage in Dudley. Speakers were selected to represent a range of social characteristics identified on the basis of ethnographic observation as likely to influence linguistic behaviour, including educational background, attitudes towards mainstream society and social networks.

It was found that all the interviewees spoke Patois in varying degrees. The relative proportions of eleven common Patois features were calculated for each of the speakers in the sample and incorporated into a frequency score. A number of statistically significant correlations were established. It was shown, for instance, that the more critical the speakers towards mainstream society, the more frequent the use of Patois was likely to be. Social network also proved to be an important explanatory variable: the more integrated into the Black community, the more frequent the use of Patois was likely to be.

There was also a statistically significant relationship between social network and two other measures of language use: Patois competence and patterns of language use. Although there was a wide variety of difference in the range of Patois features which appear in young Black people's speech, the more integrated into the Black community, the more competent their level of Patois. Similarly, those young people whose social networks were predominantly Black were more likely to use Patois features in a wider range of situations. Edwards (1986) also explores the symbolic functions of Patois usage to which we will return later.

Sebba's (1993) study based on conversational data obtained from adolescent informants in South London is significant. Young Black people were asked to tape conversations of Patois usage in their homes. He points to the use of two systems by Blacks in London which are London English and a Jamaican based creole.

Sebba is critical of the way Edwards et al (1986) obtained her data in the Dudley study. He calls the data collection controversial as informants were allowed to believe that the recorder had been switched off when it was still running, although they were told afterwards.

As a fieldworker on this project, however, I am able to confirm that most of the young people were highly amused when they discovered what had happened, none was affronted and all agreed to our use of the recorded material. Sebba's own method of data collection is also open to criticism. It is possible to argue that the idea of giving informants a tape and asking them to 'chat Patois' is flawed. For instance, did informants exaggerate their use Patois for recording purpose?

Code-Switching
We have already discussed the possibilities of describing language variation in the Caribbean and America in terms of code-switching. The case for a code-switching analysis is, however, particularly convincing when dealing with British Black speech and several recent studies have dealt with language variation in terms of two separate systems rather than a continuum. Sutcliffe (1992: 1), for example, argues that the language of the British Black community is possibly best described as two systems on the morpho-syntactic level. He uses the term British Jamaican Creole (BJC) to describe the language situation among young Black people in Britain, pointing out that:

> British Jamaican Creole (BJC) is used bilingually with standard or regional English: London English or 'Cockney' in the London area, Black Country English in the West Midlands conurbation, and so on, as a reflection of the experience of being 'Black in a White world.

Sebba (1993) also supports this notion and refers to two separate varieties, London Jamaican and London English rather than a continuum. However, it must pointed out that since there is no national and regional study of patterns of language among Black adolescents, it cannot be assumed that all young Black people in London speak a variant of Jamaican Creole. My own impression as a member of the speech community is that whilst British

Jamaican Creole is by far the most frequently used, some Black people also have access to other Caribbean creoles.

Edwards (1986: 51), suggests that the differing socio-political conditions in Britain and the Caribbean have produced quite distinct linguistic outcomes. In the Caribbean, Black people are in the majority. Inspite of the interrelation between skin colour and social status, overall social mobility is greater and more speakers have access to standard speech. In Britain, most Blacks belong to the working class: they occupy low status jobs and experience systematic discrimination. The factors which give rise to a continuum situation in the Caribbean are thus simply not present in the British context. This interpretation, she argues, is supported by the linguistic evidence. Whereas in Jamaica, basilectal and acrolectal phonology differ only in a small number of areas, the differences between regional British and Black British phonology are much more marked. In particular these varieties differ in voice set:

> The background feature of speech, including pitch, tempo, loudness and timbre are quite different for British English and West Indian varieties, so that there can seldom be any doubt as to whether a speaker is using "English" or "Patois" on phonetic criteria alone (Edwards 1986: 49).

Edwards (1986: 49) also argues that it is easier to separate the grammatical features of the different varieties in a British setting since mesolectal features tend to be less frequent in British Black speech than in Caribbean speech.

Attitude Towards Black Language
Attitudes towards Black language need to be placed within the wider context of attitudes towards the language of low status groups in general. Extensive research within sociolinguistics from the late 1960s onwards has significantly contributed to our understanding of the social and psychological processes which underlie the ways in which we evaluate speech. For some considerable time, the speech of low status groups was explained in terms of what came to be known as the deficit hypothesis. Any

71

deviations from the Standard were assumed to have resulted from inherent inadequacies. Labels like 'careless', 'slovenly' and 'lazy' were frequently attached to working class speech which was, significantly, considered to be sub-standard.

The development of sociolinguistics as an autonomous area of study in the late 1960s produced a series of important challenges to this deficit position. Writers like Labov (1969) proposed that the range of social dialects which existed within English, for instance, could best be described as *different* from the standard language, but there was no evidence to suggest that such varieties were in any way *deficient*. It became widely accepted that all non-standard varieties should be seen as perfectly regular, rule-governed language systems which fulfilled the communications needs of their speakers. The consensus among many educationalists and psychologists, influenced by the work - or the misinterpretation of the work - of Bernstein was, however, that the linguistic deficiencies associated with non-standard speech were closely linked with cognitive deficiencies and that this phenomenon offered an explanation for the poor educational achievements of dialect speakers. The difference hypothesis, however, shifted the burden of responsibility for under achievement from the dialect speakers to the school system.

Further work within the social psychology of language allowed significant insights into the ways in which we evaluate speech (of Giles & Powersland 1975: Edwards 1979; 1989). Using methodologies like the semantic differential and the matched guise techniques, it was possible to demonstrate that standard speech was evaluated positively by dialect and standard speakers alike. Standard speakers were, for instance, considered more intelligent and more competent. However, dialect speakers also associated other values with both standard and non-standard speech. Thus standard speakers were, considered to be prissy and effeminate, while dialect speech was associated with sincerity and trustworthiness. An understanding of this linguistic ambivalence is essential to an appreciation of attitudes towards Black speech in the Caribbean, America and Britain.

Attitudes towards Caribbean Language

Caribbean Creoles have a legacy of low status. Take the view expressed by Long (1774):

> The language of the Creoles is bad English larded with the Guiney dialect, owing to their adopting the African words, in order to make themselves understood by the imported slaves; which they find much easier than teaching these strangers to learn English. The better sort are very fond of improving their language by catching at any hard words that the whites happen to let fall in their hearing; and they alter and misapply it in a strange manner; but a tolerable collection of them given an air of knowledge and importance in the eyes of their brethren which tickles their vanity and makes them more assiduous in stocking themselves with this unintelligible jargon.

White, Brown and Black officials often devalued Creole and compared it unfavourably with the British standard English or the language used by the highly educated minority in the various Caribbean islands. The long term effects of negative attitudes of this kind are alive and well even in the twentieth century. Creole has frequently been dismissed as 'bad' or 'broken' and children have been warned that they will never amount to anything if they 'talk like Quashie' (Edwards 1979). The strength of feeling around this issue has often resulted in a denial of black speech patterns. Le Page (cited in Harris 1979: 25), for instance, offered the following description of reactions to a linguistic survey carried out in the Caribbean during the 1950s:

> The answer to the first question brought out at once what is obviously going to be an important factor in our survey, that is, the emotional reaction of many West Indians to any suggestion that the speech of their colony is not Standard English .. the element of despair aroused in some West Indians by what they felt to be the "bad" English spoken all around them, was difficult to eliminate from the answer.

Even in the post-independence period, the majority of the population have continued to see the relationship between standard English and African-English Creole in terms of superiority/inferiority. The views and attitudes about their use are so deeply rooted that change is likely to be a long process.

The controversy caused by the Language Arts Syllabus published by the Trinidad and Tobago Ministry of Education and Culture and discussed by Carrington & Borely (1977) is a clear example of deeply entrenched negative attitudes. The new syllabus challenged the traditional view that Black speech is slovenly and unacceptable and suggests that, since it is used almost universally by children, it should be allowed in the early years of school. A fierce debate ensued in the Trinidad press. One writer, for instance, described Trinidadian Creole as 'Trini Degenerative English'. Another person wrote:

> ... our vernacular is confidently and boldly claimed to be a total language having phonology, morphology and syntax! Conclusion ... based on premises at once so flimsy or so sterile as scarcely to merit serious consideration... I contest strongly the claim that what the child speaks in his home is not English but the vernacular. In my view it is a form of English but very bad English ... The main point of the syllabus is to encourage the child to wallow in the incorrectness and sloppiness of the vernacular (Trinidad Guardian: 28th December 1975, cited in Carrington & Borley 1977).

In spite of recent attempts that have been made in islands such as Jamaica to embrace Creole as the national language, there is no evidence to suggest any significant movement from this position in more recent times. Dodd (1993: 46), for instance, is emphatic that:

> Patois is not an African language which is preserved as Catalans preserved their language in Spain. Patois is a bastard, made up of mispronounced English words, pieces of

the Akan dialect, as well as others, mixed into a mush by usage.

In her view the examination performance is on the decline because children are not taught to use standard English. She protests against the use of Creole or Patois and sees it as a gross indictment that the average person cannot speak English. In similar vein, she berates news presenters for using 'the most clumsy Patois as if they're being funny'.

There can be little doubt as to the relative status of Creole and English in the Caribbean. English is seen as maintaining order; it is associated with decorum and authority. Creole is associated with the poor, the rural, the uneducated. Yet other forces are also at work. Creole may not have connotations of prestige or authority. It is, however, associated with sincerity, relaxation, expressiveness and involvement. Reisman (1970), in a study of Antiguan speech and society, suggests that there is evidence of a process of remodelling by which various low-status phenomena associated with Creole speech community are taken by the members of this community and attributed with positive values. Thus, Creole is described as 'broken', but speakers who 'break' into Creole are to be admired and trusted; they are underlying the very real emotions associated with the use of African-Caribbean speech patterns. This kind of linguistic schizophrenia is not, of course, limited to the Caribbean. As has already been indicated, similar reactions are to be found in many other low status groups all over the world.

Attitudes Toward Black Language in America
Attitudes towards Black English in America are very similar to those described for the Caribbean. As early as the nineteenth century Gonzales stated:

> The (Gullah) words are, of course, not African, for the African brought over or retained only a few words of his jungle-tongue, and even these few are by no means authenticated as part of original scant baggage of the negro slaves ... Slovenly and careless of speech, these Gullahs

75

seized upon the peasant English used by some of the early settlers and by the white servants of the wealthier colonists, wrapped their clumsy tongues about it as well as they could, and enriched with certain expressive African words, it is issued through their flat noses and thick lips ... With characteristic laziness, these Gullah Negroes took shorts cuts to the ears of their auditors, using as few words as possible, sometimes making one gender serve for three, one tense for several, and totally disregarding singular and plural numbers (cited in Smitherman 1977:172).

More recently negative attitudes towards Black English again became the focus of attention when writers such as Bereiter & Englemann (1966), and Jensen (1969) postulated their theories about the verbal and cognitive abilities of lower class Black children. Bereiter & Englemann in their work with four year old Black children claimed that communication was by 'gesture' and 'single words' and that the children's speech was 'a series of badly connected words or phrases' (cited in Labov 1973: 25) These deficit theorists supported the idea, that in order for children to be successful in school, they would have to acquire standard English.

During the 1970s sociolinguistic research into the language of Black children indicated that previous research based on so-called genetic inferiority (Jensen 1969) and deficient linguistic skills were dangerous on two grounds. Firstly, the deficit theorists detracted attention from the school and put the responsibility for failure on the children and their family socio-economic background. Secondly, there is no evidence to support the view that any 'normal' child could be as linguistically impaired as the deficit theorists were suggesting was the norm for the Black community. However, many educationalists accepted the deficit hypothesis and this led to a succession of compensatory education programmes designed to improve the academic performance of Black children. Not surprisingly, Black children still continued to underachieve in spite of compensatory projects such as Operation Headstart (cf Keddie 1973).

Labov's (1969) work challenged the deficit argument and demonstrated that the verbal skills of the urban Black child were in fact highly developed. The view of Labov and his supporters was that non-standard language was simply different from the standard but in no way deficient. His work was also significant because it pointed to the role of the interviewer in research. He observed that, when children are expected to perform in an asymmetrical situation with adults, their verbal behaviour is very different than when they are interacting with their peers. Children who are perceived to be 'non-verbal' by White adults in formal interview situations can be shown to be perfectly articulate in informal conversation.

There is a great deal of linguistic ambivalence towards Black English among African-Americans. For example, the writer Claude Brown (1965) comments positively about Black English in his autobiography *Manchild in the Promise Land*. Yet at the same time, when describing a court scene which involved his parents, he expresses negative feelings about their pronunciation and use of black English features.

Smitherman (1977) makes a timely contribution to the debate about deficit and difference language theories. She argues that this debate is only concerned with ideology and the norms of the White middle class and has little relevance for Black students. She claims that they do not take account of the interaction between language, school and the larger political realities of America.
Talking about Black English... without commensurably advocating changes in the socio-political system in which Black people struggle is not only short-sighted... it is an implicit acknowledgement that the system is good and valid... speaking white English is no guarantee to economic advancement. For educators, linguists, and anybody else to push that notion off on kids is to deal them a gross lie .. Meaningful and successful education for Black kids can only proceed with concomitant changes in broader educational policy and in social economic policy (1977: 207).

Attitudes Towards Black British Speech

The same negative attitudes described for African-Caribbean Creoles and African-American speech have been documented for British Black language. Edwards (1983; 1986) cites a variety of teacher sources which indicate the level of linguistic prejudice which was widespread in the early years of settlement. The Association of Teachers of English to Pupils from Overseas (ATEPO 1970), for instance, asserts that Caribbean language is "babyish, careless and slovenly, lacking proper grammar and very relaxed like the way they walk". The National Association of School Masters (NAS 1969: 5) described it as "plantation English which is socially unacceptable and inadequate for communication". They also suggested that Black children communicated by sign.

As is the case in the Caribbean and America, the Black community in Britain also express negative attitudes towards their language describing it as 'bad English' or 'broken English' (cf Harris 1979: 24). They also show a degree of linguistic ambivalence and often choose to use Patois as a symbol of group solidarity (Edwards 1986). The failure to use at least some Patois features in informal in-group situations could be misinterpreted as racial aloofness and the speaker may be branded as a snob. In informal conversation with Black people of one's own age, in contrast, the use of Patois communicates warmth, friendship and solidarity. It can also be used to reject outsiders and assert the speakers' pride in their Black identity. For instance, a young person's decision to use Patois in the classroom can sometimes be a deliberate act of defiance, a statement that they do not accept the low status which White society attaches to Black people (Edwards 1986). Young Blacks may use Patois to reject and exclude White peers, including Whites who use it when they want to identify with Black friends (cf Hewitt 1986).

Recently, there have been attempts to promote more favourable attitudes towards Black language in British schools. The growing awareness that Patois is a legitimate language system led some teachers to incorporate it into the curriculum, for instance, through poetry and drama. Sometimes attempts of this kind have been controversial. One headmaster, is reported to have said that Patois would appear on his timetable only 'over his dead body' (cf Edwards 1979). The Black community, too, have also voiced concern about the use of Patois in school by parents who feel that their children are not achieving in the British education system and also see the inclusion of Patois in the classroom as another attempt to hinder their academic performance. Many parents who have been educated in the Caribbean have been consistently told that Patois is 'bad talk' which needs to be corrected and their resistance to change is therefore, understandable. Black community activists (cf Stone 1980; Carby 1980) have also pointed to other difficulties in using Patois in school. One objection is that this is just a cosmetic exercise which does not really remove racist attitudes in school or society. As Patois is the language of resistance, to legitimise it would result in the development of new varieties which would take over the same functions. There is some indication that this is now the case (Duckett 1993).

Conclusion
Black language in the Caribbean, America and Britain can be traced directly to West Africa. During the Atlantic slave trade the deliberate policy of separating Africans who spoke the same language(s) led to the development of pidgins and creoles.

The linguistic history of Caribbean creoles is complex. While the vocabulary base in islands like Jamaica and Trinidad is predominantly English, there are many African retentions in phonology and grammar. However, the extent of African influence has been hotly debated. The current status of Caribbean speech is another topic of debate. Changes brought about by education and social and economic developments have affected patterns of use, resulting in a wide range of linguistic variations. In Jamaica, for example, this variation has been described in terms of a continuum between broad creole (or basilect) and standard Jamaican English. It has also been described as a post creole continuum, as the gap between basilect (pure Creole) and acrolect (standard Jamaican English) has narrowed. More recently writers have attempted explaining variation in terms of code-switching behaviour.

The historical development of BEV, the language used among African-Americans is similar to that of Caribbean creoles. The important difference is that in America Whites generally outnumbered Blacks, and therefore, a creole either failed to develop or rapidly underwent a process of decreolization. In America, there in disagreement as to whether Black English is currently diverging from or converging toward standard English. Given the situation of segregation and disadvantage of many African-Americans, it is highly probable that their speech patterns will continue to diverge. However, there is evidence of convergence especially in writing. The ability of African-Americans to code-switch is also an important issue.

The patterns of Black language used in Britain differ in some respects to those in the Caribbean and America. The number of Black speakers in Britain is lower than either the Caribbean or America and their presence, significantly, is more recent, dating back to the post-war period The number of British born Blacks who could speak British English led to the assumption that British Black children were losing their ability to speak Patois. Further studies indicated that this was not the case and that Black British children were able to speak Patois in varying degrees depending on a number of factors, the most important of which are the social networks of the speakers. The more integrated the speaker into the Black community, the greater the frequency of Patois usage, the higher the level of competence in Patois and the greater the number of situations in which Patois is used. The case for a code-switching analysis is particularly appropriate when dealing with Black British speech in comparison to African-American language or Caribbean creoles, because the differences between Black British and White usage is so marked.

Attitudes towards Black language should be placed within the wider context of attitudes towards the language of low status groups in general and particular attention needs to be made to the educational implications of negative attitudes. The deficit hypothesis which labelled non-standards and dialect speech as inferior was challenged by sociolinguists who viewed all deviation from the standard as different and not deficient.

Caribbean creoles have a legacy of low status and are often referred to as 'bad' or 'broken' and as the language of the poor and uneducated. However, ambivalent attitudes exist, as creoles are also associated with sincerity and relaxation. Similar kinds of negative and ambivalent attitudes can be found in Black English in America. The negative attitudes toward Black English became focused when deficit theorists postulated their views about the verbal and cognitive abilities of lower class Black children. It was later shown that the language of the urban black child was in fact highly developed. Attention has also been paid to the irrelevance of the deficit difference debate for Black speakers. Without changes in the political and social structures which oppress Black people, the educational prospects of Black children will remain poor. Similar negative attitudes have been documented for Black British speech. There have been attempts to promote more favourable attitudes towards Patois in school, however, attempts to legitimise Patois are likely to be unacceptable to parents and children as they do not solve the real educational issues.

Linguistically the development of Black language in the Caribbean is mirrored in both America and Britain, though various local conditions have given rise to many important differences. It is highly significant, however, that attitudes towards Black language closely reflect attitudes towards Black people: low status speakers are considered to have low status speech. While Black people in all three locations have internalised these negative views, the tradition of resistance has also given rise to positive views on Black speech. In all three locations, Black language is an essential element of the rich oral traditions which will be discussed in the following chapters.

CHAPTER 4

BAD TALK

ಬಿ ಬಿ ಬಿ

The focus for the next two chapters is the very wide range of speech events which occur in Black communities throughout the world and, according to many writers, separate Black speakers from White as effectively as differences in phonology and grammar (cf Kochman 1972; Reisman 1974; Abrahams 1976). An overview of this area provides a backdrop for the treatments which follow in subsequent chapters of the wide range of performative features which mark Black speech.

The definition of speech event which we use for present purposes is based on the work of Hymes (1974), Saville-Troike (1982) and others in the field of the ethnography of speaking. Saville-Troike (1982: 29), for example, defines a speech event as:

> A unified set of components throughout, beginning with the same general purpose of communication, the same general topic, and involving the same participants, generally using the same language variety, maintaining the same tone or key and the same rules for interaction, in the same setting. An event terminates whenever there is a change in the major participants, their role-relationships, or the focus of attention. If there is no change in major participants and setting, the boundary between events is often marked by a period of silence and perhaps change of body position.

The centrality of speech in Black culture is betrayed by the vast array of terms which refer to different speech events. 'Chatting', 'preaching', 'gaffing', 'mamaguy', 'labryishing', 'rapping', 'shucking', 'jiving', 'ceitfulling', 'back chatting', 'busing' (abusing), 'throwing word': these are just a small sample of the expressions used to describe a variety of verbal performances. In chapters four and five specific examples will, after Abrahams (1970), be divided into two main categories: bad talk and sweet talk. Bad talk or 'broad talk' can be defined as performances where jokes and repartee are used to draw attention to people who challenge the accepted community mores. This type of speech activity is likely to take place in contexts such as pool rooms, market places and street corners. The examples which will be considered include abuse, boasting, rap and toasting. Sweet talk, discussed in chapter five, relies on the same range of linguistic features, but is conducted in more formal and respectable settings.

'Bad Talk'

Bad talk covers an extensive range of speech events - from very strong to very mild, from playful to serious. Both adults and young people use various types of bad talk. It is very much a feature of the secular realm and is found in social activities such as 'raves', and among friends. For present purposes, we will concentrate on the better known examples of bad talk: verbal duelling, boasting, blaming, rapping and toasting.

Ritual Insults

Verbal duelling or ritual insults can be found in many Black communities. They have been documented in Africa, for instance, by Desai (1968) and Hare & Hare (1985); in America, by Labov (1977), Foster (1974) and Mitchell-Kernan (1977); in the Caribbean by Abrahams (1972b) and in England by Edwards (1979; 1986), Tomlin (1981), Sutcliffe (1982) and Saa (1985). This is an interesting area of study because it explores the creative use of language. It also throws light on many aspects of the social organisation of Black people.

The origins of verbal duelling in the diaspora lie in Africa. Institutionalised ritual insults are well-known and widely practised in many West African cultures. Hare & Hare (1985) for instance, report a Nigerian form of ritual invective called 'trickstering' whereby a boy puts down his father verbally. Similarly, Dogon men have joking relationships with their wife's sisters and their daughters (Innes 1974: 322).

They also form part of the oral tradition of Blacks in the diaspora (Levine 1977: 350). A variety of names for this speech event exist in the different Black communities. In America, it is known as 'sounding', 'screaming', 'joning', 'signifying', 'ribbin' and 'playing the dozens', depending on the geographical location. Verbal duelling can be categorised into rhymed and unrhymed. Sounding, for example, is a kind of verbal duel built on unrhymed exchanges. There is a requirement that the reply must be appropriate, well structured and built on the particular model offered. Take the following example of sounding cited in Folb 1980: 92).

A: Yey man, you look like a goddam Christmas tree!
You a regular caution sign! You righteously light
up the whole street!

B.   Listen sucker, don't be buyin' my clothes in
Woolworths like some five-and-dime nigger-five
cen fo' yo' shirt an' 'dime fo' yo'n pants!

The idea of the game is to hurl quick jokes back and forth in an attempt to beat your opponent. The second speaker takes up the theme of appearance, offered by the first, but develops it in a new direction.

Closely related to sounding is its rhymed equivalent, 'playing the dozens' (cf Dollard 1939; Abrahams 1970c). A further distinction can be made between the 'dirty dozens' with explicit sexual overtones, particularly related to one's mother and the clean dozens (Folb 1980). However, the term 'dozens' seems to be disappearing. Other names include: 'checking', 'crackin' and 'getting on moms' (Dandy 1991). As is the case in sounding, insults are hurled back and forth between opponents. Examples are reported by Labov (1977: 308):

> However, the need to build on the insult offered by the previous speaker is less urgent in playing the dozens than in sounding. The most impressive player is the one with the biggest stock of rhymed couplets: the need is more for good memory and quick delivery than skill.

The American literature tends to focus on verbal duelling among adolescents, although there is also some reference to adults. In most cases, discussion focuses on males but there is some evidence of female involvement. Edwards & Sienkewicz (1990) draw attention to several writers who explore verbal duelling in young women including H Rap Brown (1969) and Ladner (1972).

In the Caribbean, a form of verbal duelling similar to playing the dozens is known variously as 'rhyming', 'giving rag', 'making mock' or 'fatiguing'. In the following example reported by Abrahams (1972b: 224-5), a group of six adolescent males from Tobago, compete in a ongoing stream of rhymes:

1. Ten pound iron, ten pound steel. ...
2. I put your mother to back o' train.
3. Christmas comes but once a year.
4. Ten crapaud [inedible frogs] was in a pan; ...
5. If aeroplane was not flying in the air, ...
6. If snake was not crawlin' on the ground
    [pronounced grung] ...
7. Beep bop, what is that? ...
8. Beep bop, what is that? ...
9. Tee-lee-lee tee-lee-lee, what is that? ...
10. Voo, voo, what is that? ...

It is interesting to note, too, that the tradition of ritual insults has been maintained by many second and third generation children of Caribbean descent in Britain. In England, 'running down', 'messing' 'dis'/'dissin' (an abbreviation for 'disrespect') are some of the words used by young people to date to describe this speech event. Words like 'dis' can also be found among African-Americans (cf Hooks 1993). It would appear that such terms are transmitted through African-American music culture and television programmes such as 'The Fresh Prince of Bel Air', which have exerted a great deal of influence on young Blacks in England.

Edwards (1979: 50) points to evidence of emergent duelling behaviour among children as young as 10 years of age. On some occasions, insults are rhymed as can be seen in the following example:

Plain!

A:	Hush you mouth
B:	Why should I
A:	Cos it's closing time
B:	But I ain't a shop, so!
A:	I said, shut you mouth
B:	Why should I?
A:	Cos you lip long like frog
B:	You don't talk about you own lip do you?
A:	You mouth favour the dog.
B:	A dog can eat off a frog! So!
A:	But a frog can jump over a dog! So!
B:	Take a mash and don't come flash! Take the shame and don't complain!

On other occasions, they are more reminiscent of the North American sounding. My own recordings includes the following examples:

Sonia: What happen shortie? Gosh you're tiny like
Tiny Tim.
Norma: At least I'm not fat and my clothes fit me and I haven't got any tyres on my body.
Sonia: Well I'm not a bag of bones and there's something to hold.

Audience participation is an essential aspect of these verbal exchanges in all the geographical contexts discussed above. Members of the audience often act as catalysts for competition by using such remarks as:

'You tell him' or,
'What she going on with?' (What is she talking about?)

They show their approval or disapproval, as the contest develops and, if one of the players is defeated, a member of the audience may step in to replace them. Audience interaction is a theme to which we will return in chapter six.

Although ritual invective has its roots in oral culture, its influence can also be detected in the written literature of Black communities. Take, for instance, the work of Louise Bennett (1966: 28). In the following poem the professional charm of the local candy-seller in Jamaica is skilfully turned into abrasive humour at the expense of reluctant or unwilling customers:

Candy lady, candy mam?
Bizniz bad now a days
Lady wid de pretty lickle bwoy
buy candy, gwan yu ways!
You right fe draw de pickney han,
koo pon him nose hole,
him y'eye dem a-tare out like him want
hickmatize me candy-bole.

[Candy lady, candy madam?
Business is not that good
The lady with the pretty little boy
buy some candy, and be on your way!
Your right to hold your child's hand
look at the size of his nostrils
look at his eyes, they are staring as if he wants
to hypnotise my candy bowl]

Functions of Ritual Invective

Ritual invective serves a number of important functions in Black communities. It allows participants to defuse potentially explosive situations through humour; it provides a means for establishing one's place in the pecking order; it entertains and, at the same time, is intellectually stimulating; it also give important insights into the cultural values of the group.

Verbal duels are ritual not real and are always mediated by an audience. In situations which might easily degenerate into violence and unpleasantness, exchanges such as those described in the preceding pages act as a kind of steam-valve for aggression. Humour is used to lower the temperature, to defuse the potential for violence.

The importance of ritual invective as a form of social control should not, however, detract from a range of other functions, including its potential to entertain the crowd. Good verbal duelling is fast, competitive and highly interactive and the style of delivery is every bit as important as the message. Young Black people play endless games with each other and words are tools for power and personal gain. Because verbal excellence is recognized as an important and powerful way of manipulating others, the good talker has a highly prized position in Black society. Verbal games, such as playing the dozens are, in many ways, examples of manipulative behaviour. By ousting an opponent through the force of your joke or insult, you have established your social superiority over that person. However, as Hannerz (1969: 85) points out:

> All prestige accrued from being a good talker does not have to do with the strictly utilitarian (manipulative) aspect. A man with a good repartee in arguments is certain to be appreciated for his entertainment value, and those men who can talk about the high and the mighty, people and places, and the state of the world, may stake claims to a reputation of being heavy 'upstairs'.

Ritual invective also underlines the cultural values of the community. Many of the insults, observed among Black people in the diaspora, are about physical appearance, with particular emphasis on skin tone, nose and the mouth. For example, 'yu lip long like hog' (Your lips are as long as a pig's) or 'Yu black like pat ' (You are as black as a pot). Ritual insults, rhymed or unrhymed, also make use of simile, metaphor and hyperbole, as can be seen in the following example of a Jamaican woman residing in England:

> What you have on you favour when fowl a lay egg
> [Your clothes make you look like a chicken laying an egg]
> or:
> Your hair is like a crocus bag, your skin is like a grater

Mitchell-Kernan and Kernan (1977) find African-American children's insults focus mainly on appearance and intellectual ability. Rowe (personal communication), too, has noted the references and comments made about appearance by Black children and adolescents in Britain. Names such as 'bone head', 'moonhead', 'spaceman', 'bricky', 'bun up bacon' (burnt bacon) to describe physical characteristics are common.

Ever since the days of slavery and early European contact with Africans, negroid features have been caricatured by Whites, and writers such as Wesling (1986) have commented on the ways in which Black people have tended to internalize the negative views of the colonizers. Others, however, have questioned this interpretation. Reisman (1970), for instance, points to ways in which Black people have consistently 'remodelled' the negative values attached to Black culture and society, reinterpreting them in a positive way. Thus the word 'nigger' is used widely among African-Americans but appears not to have negative connotations. It seems that references to physical attributes in verbal duelling should not necessarily be taken at face value.

There has also been a great deal of discussion of the social meanings attached to the obscenity which is a recurrent feature of verbal duelling (cf Henderson 1973: 35), (Hannerz 1969: 130).

Various explanations have been postulated for this phenomenon. Dollard (1939), for instance, has suggested that playing the dozens provides an outlet for Black people's anger at their oppression by White people. According to Wesling (1986), ever since the days of slavery, Black men were not allowed to call themselves 'men' but were referred to as boys: only the White slave master was known as 'the man'. Consequently, Black men and women use the term 'baby' to describe Black men. As Wesling says in her lecture delivered at Brent Town Hall in London, 1986:

> The Black man call himself baby. The woman he sleeps with mamma calls the place he sleeps a crib (a cradle).

Abrahams (1962) argues that this phenomenon is a male ritual which reflects the tensions caused by the so-called matriarchal or 'absent father' household. He also points out that the insertion of the first-person pronouns and the close identification of the speaker with unreal situations are an expression of male sexual identity (1970: 164). However, Edwards & Sienkewicz (1990: 120) suggest that these various explanations are unconvincing. As previously noted, women also play the dozens and they often use the same kinds of obscenities as their male counterparts. Nor should we lose sight of the fact that the preoccupation with the mother is also practised in societies that are not necessarily matrifocal (Dundes et al 1972). The interpretation of obscenities in verbal duelling thus remains a subject of debate. What is beyond question, however, is the centrality of this speech event as a source of entertainment and as a means by which young performers can develop verbal skills which establish a place for themselves in the pecking order.

Boasting

Boasting is another example of a bad-talking speech event which has been widely reported in Black communities and has its origins in Africa. Once more, the terminology for this event varies from place to place. In Nigeria, for example the phrase 'get mouth' is used to describe a person who boasts; in Belize and Jamaica, the term 'bose' is used; in America the same speech event is known as "woofin" (wolfing). In England, Black British young people also use the term 'bose' or 'boastful'. In all cases, it is a form of behaviour which is strongly associated with young Black males.

Boasts are a part of the African oral culture. In title-taking ceremonies among the Igbo of Nigeria, for instance, self-praises are chanted by the celebrant or by a masquerade performing on the celebrant's behalf. Take the following boast recorded by Egudu et al (1971) and cited in Okpewho (1992: 122).

I am
tiger that defends neighbours
King that is liked by public
Fame that never wanes
Flood that can't be impeded
Ocean that can't be exhausted
Wealth that gives wisdom.

The same tradition of boasting is evident in the Mandinka legend and oral epic based on Sunjata, a powerful and fearless warrior who rescued his people from the tyranny of a foreign usurper, Sumanguru. In Dembo Kanute's song, for instance, Faa Koli, Sunjata's chief lieutenant, challenges Sumanguru's generals with the following boast:

I have sworn an oath by all the men and women of Manding that tomorrow. Tomorrow when we meet at Kaya - Great Jibirila, Sumanguru's senior commander,
Has among his followers ten men.
He has ten followers who are learning to acquire supernatural powers;
Those ten men are his followers;
Those who are his followers,
Tomorrow I will catch every one of them with my bare hands,
I will not take a sword, I will not take anything,
I will punch them all with my fist,
And kill the lot of them.

(Innes 1974: 663 cited in Edwards & Sienkewicz 1990: 105).

Boasting is a powerful performance strategy which, like ritual invective, requires an audience. There is, however, a clear distinction between boasting in the public arena and more informal exchanges where the speaker proclaims his or her virtues and is likely to provoke mild dislike. As the Jamaican proverb makes clear, "self-praise is no recommendation". In general, though, boasting is not taken too seriously. Take the following example reported recently by a young Black professional woman in England:

> I thank God I have a good brain.
> In the mouth of a white speaker, such a boast might be felt to be, at best, inappropriate and, at worst, extremely arrogant. Within the Black community, however, boasts of this kind are perceived as a gentle and totally acceptable form of self-assertion.

Boastful behaviour can be used to devastate enemies. It often fulfils an important psychological function as a form of defence against criticism. The person who responds to a physical challenge with a boast, shows their strength in a more effective way than if, for instance, they had matched force with force.

This type of 'bad talk' however, is nearly always misinterpreted by outsiders. Mohammed Ali perplexed White people by his declaration that he was 'the greatest'. His rhymes often predicted the demise of his opponents. It is noticeable, though, that many aspects of his delivery underlined that he was not operating in the arena of normal conversational exchanges. The fact that his predictions were often made in rhyme - 'Sonny Liston is great/But he'll fall in eight' (cited in Toop 1984: 29) - makes it clear that we are dealing here with a special speech event. Like the heroes of the African epic Sunjata, Ali was setting out to undermine his opponent with the power of his words.

It is also important to remember that Ali's boasts did not take place in a cultural vacuum. Boasting is a widespread speech event in Black communities and, on occasions, has been developed to an art form. Take for instance, the Caribbean calypso (Warner-Lewis 1979: 112):

Are you a madman, a fool, or a stranger
To enter into this source of danger?
I am praised in the superlative degree
I sat down men on their bended knee
And teach them not to tamper with me
For my constitution
Is made up of an iron barication
San dimanite

The calypso originated from slave songs brought by West Africans to the Caribbean in the early 1600s. It mainly developed in Trinidad but has spread to other Caribbean islands such as Barbados. The songs provide social commentary on a wide range of issues and function as a powerful political weapon. The calypso has enjoyed great popular appeal. As in other speech events, the entertainment value is high; the audience take pleasure in the exaggerated claims of the performer and are fully in tune with any political point he might be making. Such an approach has much to recommend itself over more direct and serious attacks, either verbal or physical.

Blame

Blaming, unlike boasting is essentially an act of criticism aimed at individuals and is often confrontational. Similar names for this speech event exist in diverse Black communities. For instance, in West Africa and the Caribbean it is known as 'abusing' or 'cursing' and in Britain it is also referred to as 'cursing'.

Reprimanding behaviour, where negative references are made to individuals is often satirical. Songs of personal abuse or lampoons are widespread in Africa. Take the following song from the Igbo of eastern Nigeria deploring the decline in educational standards among the Youth:

We know how to speak English
We know how to speak Igbo

Why are school boys of today so ignorant?
You test them in Igbo they fail
You test them in English they fail
The school fees we pay are wasted
"Bongo" trousers have ruined them
"Bongo" trousers have ruined them
(Nwogo 1981: 237 cited in Okpewho 1992: 149).

Floppy, bell-bottomed (bongo) trousers were in fashion among young men in Nigeria in the 1960s and 1970s. According to the song, this mode of fashion has turned the young people away from the pursuit of education.

Blaming behaviour between individuals is also a common activity, both in Africa and the diaspora. Guyanese busin', for example, takes place when one's participant considers that the other has shown disrespect for ones social rights and privileges. It is often conducted among women who know each other well. Take the following abuse of a landlady towards her tenant who refused to pay the rent, recorded by Kean Gibson (cited in Edwards 1978: 203-204):

> Brin mi moni, brin mi moni ar muv out me ples. E gone her from you, you blasted tif, de spenin di moni at pi-ets-gi. Yu raidin hai; a gon her bout yu. You raidin hai, bot yu mos raid kerfuli!

(Bring my money. Bring my money or move out my place. I gon hear from you, you blasted thief, spending the money at P.H.G.

[Public Hospital, Georgetown]. You're riding high; I gon hear about you. You are riding high, but you must ride carefully.

The success of this exchange depends on the knowledge shared by members of the community that women only visit the Public Hospital, in Georgetown (P.H.G.) regularly if they have a social disease and that a woman who is 'riding high' (enjoying high living) is invariably earning her money immorally. The most important feature of busin' is its truth value or plausibility.

Busin' can sometimes be used as a strategy to clear the air and provide the basis for renewed friendship. The presence of an audience, composed of relatives and neighbours is important. Often a member of the audience intervenes to avoid the busin' session from escalating into physical assault. The main function of busin is to maintain social equilibrium.

Rapping and Toasting

Both boasting and blaming are also frequent features of two related Black speech events, rapping and toasting. I turn my attention first to rapping, an African-American word for talking, which was first used to describe a kind of African-American popular music in the 1970s. It consists of rhythmic talk over music and involves a disc jockey (known as a DJ) and a master of ceremony (MC) working in unison; the DJs provide the musical accompaniment and the MCs create spoken rhymes, catch phrases and commentaries on a variety of subjects, ranging from sex to politics. The Jamaican born Clive Campbell (known as Kool Here) is thought to be the first modern rapper. Other pioneers include Afrika Bambaataa and Grand master Flash (Morley 1992).

Rap was, in turn, a development of Hip-Hop, a musical event with clear links to a West African past. Toop (1984: 8) describes this development in the following terms:

The first so-called rap records were in fact the tip of the iceberg - under the surface was a movement called hip hop, a Bronx-based sub culture, and beneath that was a vast expanse of sources reaching back to West Africa. The praise song, social satires and boasting of Savannah Griots that appeared to reincarnate in groups had all been present in black music over the last 80 years.

Rap can take various forms including fast rap, and is often so rapid in delivery that words and meaning are unintelligible to the outsider. Interestingly, this type of fast rapping also exists in Africa. The praise poems among the Akan of Ghana, for example, are half spoken and half sung at high speed, "the emphasis being on the continual flow of utterances which need not be linked by any apparent intellectual thread" (Nketia 1979: 23-25).

Although rap is mainly dominated by African-American men such as Ice T and NWA (Niggers with an attitude), there are many Black British male rap artists such as Stone Love and Body Guard. The emergence of rap has also featured many Black women rap artists, for example, Queen Latifah, Yo-Yo and Salt 'N Pepper in America and Monie Love and the Cookie Crew in Britain. White rap artists such as Vanilla Ice from America and MC Tunes from Britain have also attracted popular acclaim.

The Jamaican verbal art of 'toasting' is similar to rap but is strongly linked to reggae music which has its roots in the days of slavery but evolved in its present form in the West Kingston slums in the mid 1960s (Johnson 1982). Ragga music, in turn, is a derivation of reggae which often contains sexually explicit language known as 'slackness'. Toasting here should not be confused with the Black narrative toasts of urban America such as 'The Signifying Monkey' (cf Abrahams 1970b).

In the same way as the American MCs, DJs in Jamaica, such as the famous Count Machuky started using the microphone to talk over reggae records. This became formalized when performers such as Big Youth and Al Capone began producing records. Toasting was performed over the B side of records, the instrumental rhythm track of side A, and became known as the 'dub version'. The culture of toasting spread rapidly in Britain. Sound systems, or mobile discotheques, were very important in its popularization. Groups of young people, known as 'posse', would build up their own sound system, give it a name like Body Guard, Yard Love and Positive Vibes and play at social events like parties and small clubs. Toasts are performed by one or more of the members of a group (Hewitt 1986).

Like its rap counterpart, toasting is mainly performed by men such as Chaka Demus and Buju Banton, but there are also female toasters, such as Sophie George and Ranking Miss P. Toasting enjoys a following not only in Jamaica but in Britain and

America. Like rap, it appeals to Black and White audiences. Smiley Culture's song 'Cockney Translation', for instance, was an attempt to translate for the White record-buying public the meaning of certain important phrases:

Cockney have names like Arthur and Tell boy. We have names
like Winston, Lloyd and Leroy.
Cockney say 'jam', we live ina 'yard'
Cockney say 'shooter' we 'bus gun'
Cockney say 'terrific' we say 'gwaan'
Cockney say 'ole bill' we say 'dotty Babylon'...

(cited in Jah Bones 1986: 65-66)

Both toasting and rapping incorporate a wide range of stylistic devices such as repetition, which will be discussed in later chapters. They also share certain elements with other Black speech events. For instance, ritual invective is a frequent feature of both rap and toasts.

Performers often challenge each other to see who can 'chat the baddest lyrics' (produce the best lyrics). There is much improvisation. It can be argued that toasting and rapping enable young Black people to channel their creative energy by engaging in a contest of words. As is the case in ritual invective, the role of the audience is critical and they are often given an opportunity to perform. They respond in a variety of ways to the performer. They sing, repeat key words or phrases of a song, cheer or chant, for example 'oh-oh, oh-oh'. They also talk back in response to the performer's question, 'Are you ready?' or 'Is there anybody in the house?' Call- response behaviour of this kind will be dealt with in greater detail in chapter six.

A form of toasting known in Britain as deejaying, is, like fast rap, extremely fast in delivery and covers a range of topics. Toasts, like rap, covers a range of topics. Some songs are social commentaries and thus often have a political theme. For example, the following song by Supercat exhorts young people to deal with their oppression.

98

Get up, stand up,
stand up for your right
me sey get up stand up
me sey yout men don't give up de fight
little-little-little yout
stand up for you right, little yout man
get up stand up
for me sey don't give up de fight
You can fool some a de you dem some time
but you can't fool all de yout dem all de time
and now de yout dem see de light

Some artists, such as Public Enemy, as well as covering a range of political topics, are especially concerned with raising the level of consciousness amongst Black people of their social circumstances. Such songs known as 'consciousness rap' are becoming increasingly popular. The following song, entitled 'Shut 'Em Down', basically condemns White ownership of businesses in Black areas:

I testified my mamma cried
Black people died
When the other man lied
See listen to me double trouble
I overhaul and I'm comin' from the lower level
I'm takin' tabs
Sho nuff stuff to grab
Like shirts it hurts
Wit neck to wreck
Took a poll 'cause our soul
Took a toll
From the education
Of a TV station
But look around
Hear go the sound of the wreckin' ball
Boom and pound

When I shut 'em down
I shut 'em down shut 'em down, shut 'em shut 'em down
I shut 'em down ...

While much rapping and toasting centres on political questions of
this kind, it must also be noted that a great deal of energy is
focused on the same kind of sexist and macho boasting which
characterises the verbal duelling discussed above. Interestingly,
however, women rappers and toasters often openly challenge this
sexism and sexual harassment contained in the so-called 'slack' or
'gangster rap' songs that are sexually explicit (Turner 1991: 61).
The following song from Salt 'N Pepper, entitled 'Tramps' deals
with women's unwanted attention from men:

Tramps
Tramps
Home girls attention you must hate
so listen close to what I say
don't take this as a simple rhyme
cause this type of thing happens all the time

What would you do
if a stranger said ahah
would you dis (disrespect) him
or would you reply
that you will become a victim of circumstances...

You are what you are
I am what I am
it just so happens
that most men are tramps

Conclusion
Black speech events in the diaspora can be divided into two main
categories: bad talk and sweet talk. In the present chapter, the
focus has been on bad talk those performances where less
respectable members of the group challenge the accepted
community values.

Bad talk takes on a variety of forms: the verbal duelling of young people, especially though not exclusively of young men; the boasting of the calypso; the blaming behaviour of women who seek redress; the raps and toasts of DJs and their sound system.

Such 'broad talking' serves an equally wide range of functions. It usually takes place within a public forum in which the audience acts as adjudicator and makes it possible to defuse potentially explosive situations. It allows performers to establish their place in the pecking order of the group. It restores the social equilibrium. It entertains and it provides important insights into the cultural values of the group.

CHAPTER 5

SWEET TALK

ಶ್ರ ಶ್ರ ಶ್ರ

A s we have seen in chapter four, verbal display is an important part of speech events in many Black communities. Bad or 'broad talkers' have various opportunities to exercise their verbal skills using language which is sometimes licentious or which challenges the status quo. Sweet talk, on the other hand, is respectable in content and context, and has a different function from that of bad talk. For instance, the philosophy of the Limba people of Sierra Leone is that 'ghonkoli', or 'good speaking both influences social outcomes and maintains harmony (cf Finnegan 1988).

The most obvious example of 'good talk' is the oratory that is to be found in a wide variety of settings, from the law courts of West Africa to the sermons of Black preachers and the political speeches of Black activists. Other examples of good talk on which I will draw in the pages which follow include the storytelling activities of a wide range of Black communities in Africa, America, the Caribbean and Britain.; and dub poetry, a sweet talking act with many resonances of the rap and toasting discussed in the previous chapter. To begin, however, I will explore the role of 'throwing word', which has received relatively little attention and which has the potential to straddle both sweet talk and bad talk.

Throwing Word

'Throwing words' involves the use of indirect language to slander or reprimand someone, often in a humorous manner, and is an important example of 'sweet talk' in many Black communities. In Nigerian Pidgin English the term used for this speech event is 'yapping'. In America, it is known as 'signifying', in Jamaica as 'throwin word' or 'droppin remarks' and in Belize as 'throwing a phrase' (cf Kernan et al 1977). The Guyanese equivalent is 'tantalizin' (Edwards 1979: 85), whereas in Barbados this speech event is known as 'dropping remarks' (Callender 1990). Blacks in Britain also use the term 'throwin word' or 'droppin remarks'.

Signifying, in America, is used in a wide variety of contexts. Indirect remarks, often caustic in effect, are intended to send a clear message. For example, Kwame Ture, the Black political activist of the 1960s, addressing a white audience at the University of California-Berkeley in 1966, is reported to have said:

> It's a privilege and an honour to be in the white intellectual ghetto of the West (cited in Smitherman 1977: 120).

This use of language is in marked contrast to that of the verbal duellers which was discussed in the previous chapter. Ritual invective is full of exaggerated language, often obscene, and achieves the desired effect by breaking all the norms of 'polite' discourse. Signifying, in contrast, makes use of irony and understatement. By expressing one's views about matters which are often of great consequence in a quiet, low key way, the speaker achieves a humorous disjunction.

Sometimes, as in the case of Ture, the target is the political status quo. On other occasions, the speaker focuses on people and events rather nearer home. Edwards (1979: 86), for instance, describes how Elsa, a Guyanese woman, hands placed on hips, stares specifically at a new pair of shoes worn by one member of the group:

(eh-eh child, I notice somebody visited Bat. [a shoe store] yesterday).

Normally, this kind of speech behaviour has a regulative function. The teasing of a friend about some infringement of the social norms inadvertently serves as a reminder of the values the friend has violated. It would appear that the wearing of a new pair of shoes by Elsa's friend has been interpreted as ostentatious, a value not generally encouraged. The humour inherent in the delivery, however, makes it difficult for the target to take offence. The use of indirect language, instead of challenging or causing offence, defuses the situation and can have the effect of reinforcing the bonds of friendship.

Throwing words or 'droppin remarks' can also take place out of earshot of the individual at whom it is being directed, especially if the person is not a friend. Christine Callender and Adrian Humphrey, two Black British young people, illustrate this kind of behaviour in an interview with Attila the Stockbroker in the Radio 4 programme, 'The Art of Insult'. In the following example, they describe a man who is proud of the clothes he wears even though they are far too tight for him. The irony is that he cannot afford to pay the baker for his daily deliveries even though he is 'styling' (showing off):

Adrian:	Look at he going down de road like he styling
Christine:	Ah ah he owe de bread man money
Adrian:	Yeah you could tell by his shirt tight tight tight and look at his pants too
Christine:	hmhm.

Throwing words is also a vehicle for the display of verbal eloquence and wit. The speaker shows originality and humour, qualities which possibly explain why this strategy is used frequently in both sacred and secular contexts. Speakers who throw words score points not by using licentious language but by understatement or indirect comments on their target.

Throwing words can be found in a wide range of settings. Pentecostal Preachers, for instance, sometimes engage in this behaviour as a means of exerting their power and controlling members who deviate from the norms and values of the Church. Take this rebuke offered by a pastor in a Church in West Yorkshire who was making specific reference to the young people who had attended a church event elsewhere and consequently were not able to support their own local service:

Up and down
up and down
you young people
like to go up and down

We are dealing, then, with a speech event which wavers precariously between good talk and bad and which can be used to equal effect by the street wise youth and the preacher in his pulpit.

Oratory

In Black communities in Africa, the Caribbean, America and Britain, a wide range of speech events are conducted in formal settings which allow speakers to show off their verbal skills. Abrahams (1972a) describes as 'sweet talkers' performers who use rhetoric to emphasise decorum and moral values. Sermons, testimonies, speechmaking in weddings and political speeches are forms of oratory which regularly mark important social occasions.

Oratory in a Sacred Context

The church is a powerful institution in Black culture and offers an important platform for the development and display of oratorical skills. Smitherman (1977: 90) describes the sacred style of Black churches in America as :

> That in which the content and religious substance has been borrowed from Western Judaeo-Christian tradition but the communication of that content - the process - has remained essentially African.

This description applies equally to Black churches in the Caribbean and Britain. The verbal skills of Black preachers have been well documented. They are discussed in Africa, for instance, by Shorter (1974); in the Caribbean by Barrett (1976); in America by Mitchell (1970; 1990), Davis (1985) and Rosenberg (1988); and in Britain by Sutcliffe & Tomlin (1986) and Callender & Cameron (1990).

While the oratorical skills of Black preachers have been widely reported in charismatic and Pentecostal churches, such skills are also to be found in Black preachers in various other denominations. For instance, Wilkinson (1993) reports that some Anglican parishioners in Birmingham believe that Black Anglican preachers have a more powerful delivery than their White counterparts. However, Black Pentecostal churches are particularly distinctive because both the preacher and congregation participate in all parts of the service. Members are given the opportunity to preach or give a mini-sermon known as an 'exhortation'. The qualifications for exhortation are not dependent on age or sex but on ability and spiritual maturity.

Black preachers are expected to be excellent orators. Sermons are dynamic in delivery and good preachers are able to captivate their audience with their wide range of verbal skills. Although many preachers prepare their sermons in that they study the bible and biblical commentaries, they depend mainly on divine guidance to lead them and do not adhere to a prepared text. Preaching is characterised by a range of verbal devices, including improvisation, call and response, repetition, oral narrative and proverbial expressions, which will be discussed in greater detail in chapters six and seven.

The context in which most speech events takes place is often fixed and associated with specific structures. This is particularly true of Black Pentecostal Church services in Africa, America, the Caribbean and Britain. There is a high degree of extemporization and improvisation within a very well-defined and rigid structure, not always apparent to the outside. The main speech events within this context are preaching, testimony and prayer. The service is chaired by a 'moderator'. The morning service usually begins with a prayer, followed by a 'devotional' which consists of singing, a bible reading and congregational prayer; the choir sings, notices are given; the sermon follows. Invariably an 'altar call' is made whereby those who are not 'saved' or committed Christians are invited to join 'the faith' by standing or kneeling in front of the altar. Christians are often invited to 'come to the altar' to pray for a particular or specific situation. The highlight of the service, however, is the sermon, usually delivered by the pastor, though sometimes by other individual members. This event will be discussed in greater detail in chapters six and seven. For the present, I will focus on testimony, the speech event in which all members of the congregation are particularly encouraged to participate.

Testimonies

Testimonies form a part of the evening service in a traditional Black Pentecostal Church. The moderator usually begins this part of the service with a 'lively chorus'. These are very well known short songs, which have a rapid tempo and are sung from memory over and over again. Testimonies are offered by members who tell of God's goodness, divine visitation and their own spiritual experiences. They follow a particular format. Usually the person who testifies begins with "Shall we praise the Lord?" This formula may be repeated several times as the emotional or spiritual tempo increases. Often the testifier quotes from a verse of a song or the Bible. Take the following testimony by Sister Smith, New Testament Church of God (Dudley):

Shall we praise the Lord?
Shall we praise the Lord again?
I thank God for saving my soul.
I thank God for making me whole.
As the song writer says,
What can wash away my sins?
Nothing but the blood of Jesus.
What can make me whole again?
Nothing but the blood of Jesus.
And tonight I thank God for the blood of Jesus.

Sometimes, the testifier, sings a verse of a song which is in line with their testimony. For example:

I sing because I'm happy
I sing because I'm free
Praise God my doubts are settled
and I know he watches me.

Testifying is an important aspect of Black Pentecostal culture and illustrates the communal and interactive nature of Black verbal culture. Indeed expressing one's thoughts and emotions in a public arena is an accepted part of Black oral tradition (cf Kochman 1981).

The themes which emerge in testimonies include: salvation, life health and God's goodness. Sometimes the devil's ploys are mentioned, followed by an explanation of how God has complete 'victory'; thus the phrase 'I thank God for the victory we have in Him' is often used. Black Pentecostals see the conflict between good and evil, God and Satan, as a very real 'battle', symbolic of their physical and spiritual existence. Both sermons and testimonies incorporate the theme of human sin which can only be eradicated through faith in God.

Weddings
The same verbal fluency which accompanies oratory in a sacred context is to be found in a variety of other sacred and secular contexts including weddings and engagement celebrations. Enormous importance is given to speechmaking in engagements and wedding ceremonies in many Black communities. In Nigeria, for example, professional orators are employed at the engagement ceremony which involves the gathering of the two families. The ceremony itself is elaborate; so, too, are the speeches. Similarly, the Limba people of Sierra Leone regard marriage negotiations as a semi-public transaction. The suitor is often represented by a friend who must speak pleasingly in order to win the hearts of his future in-laws and impress them by showing respect. The father of the woman must thank them gracefully. For example:

I thank you. I thank you for coming. Greetings for undergoing the journey. Greetings for the sun. Greetings for the rain. I, the father of the girl, I have no long words to say (Finnegan 1970: 453).

Weddings are important community events throughout the diaspora and it is not unusual in Britain, for example, to have up to 400 guests. Although many Black people, have inherited the Western Judaeo-Christian tradition and the ceremony follows the usual Christian patterns, there is tremendous variation in the marriage ceremony itself. The bridal party for instance may march in using complicated foot movements or the bride may enter whilst the saxophonist is playing.

After the ceremony, there is always an address. Take the following, delivered by Reverend Joel Edwards at the marriage of Dawn and Ian Lewinson in the New Testament Church of God, Willesden London, October 1991:

> God designed marriages. You know they say marriages are made in heaven. I'm not quite sure about that. Maybe, if they are, they're assembled on earth. After you leave the altar there is still a lot of work to be done. So maybe if they are made in heaven, they shouldn't be seen as Scandinavian pine furnishing, you know, which comes expensive and ready made, I think a feel of MFI stuff. Not because it's cheap but after you bought this stuff you have to go home and put it together. That is the challenge that comes to us today. You have to go home and be ready to get down on your knees and look at the instructions together carefully and put it together.

Reverend Edwards uses a typical Christian theme, the sacred nature of marriage, and examines its practical implications. He extends upon the popular adage that 'marriages are made in heaven but lived on earth' by drawing upon the analogy of self-assembled furniture. This kind of imagery, in which the everyday and mundane are juxtaposed with the spiritually elevated and removed, is typical of Black Pentecostal delivery.

He continues his address by looking at the issue of mental strength in marital relationships:

> This tremendous mystery of God, how two people can become one still fascinates me. I heard a quote from Mother Bell from COGIC [Church of God in Christ] one time. She was contemplating who was stronger than whom in a marriage relationship and she came up with a tremendous word of inspiration. I hope it was original because it was really good and she said. 'Now we really know who is stronger than whom don't we because when you look at it, man was made out of dust but woman was made out of bone. We often use bones to beat down dust [audience roars with laughter] but what God has given us in our union together is not a licence but love.

Again, he uses the powerful imagery of bones and dust to convey who has the real strength in the relationship. Reverend Edwards, like many Black preachers, uses imagery as an important teaching point.

However, it is not only preachers who display their oratorical skills on occasions such as these. Abrahams (1970a: 524) gives an example of a highly elaborate speech delivered by a guest at a wedding, in Nevis in the Caribbean. The orator, makes a wide range of allusions to the Bible and makes use of Latin or latinate expressions:

> As I stand on this happy occasion giving my best wishes to all Mr. Bride and Mrs. Bride - when I look around at this domicile it makes me feel 'Homa Doma' which is to say it makes me feel like a new girl. Mr. and Mrs Bride, this feast reminds me of the feast of Belshazzar ... Ima dance 'pase ar de boca' come and take - a kiss from the lips all time touch the heart.

Such flowery language is often greeted with embarrassment by Western observers and dismissed as obsequious. There is evidence that this has long been the case. A well-documented example of such cross-cultural misunderstanding concerns the contact between European planters in the Caribbean and West African slaves. The views of Bryan Edwards (1793: 78-9), for instance, on the verbal skills of the slaves were typical of Europeans during that time:

> Among other propensities and qualities of the Negroes must not be omitted their loquaciousness. They are as fond of exhibiting set speeches, as orators by profession; but it requires a considerable patience to hear him throughout; for they commonly make a long preface before they come to the point; beginning with a tedious enumeration of their past services and hardships. They dwell with particular energy (if the fact admits it) on the number of children they have presented to Massa (Master). Yet I have sometimes heard them convey strong meaning in a narrow compass: I have been surprised by such figurative expressions, (and notwithstanding their ignorance of abstract terms) such pointed sentences, as would reflect no disgrace on poets and philosophers.

There is a well-documented history of praise songs and poetry in Africa which has clearly influenced public performances of this kind. In the following praise poem, for instance, the well-known performer from Mali, Seydou Camara pays tribute to his generous patron, who normally goes hunting bare-bodied:

Naked Buttock Battler and
Naked Chest Battler.
Look to the Green Head Smasher
for the Green Eye Gouger.
You who have offered me a skull
As a face-washing bowl,
And offered me a skin
As a covering cloth.
You have given me a great tongue
So that I may speak to the world.
The brave offered me fresh blood

As face-washing water,
And gave me a tail
As a hut-sweeping broom
And offered me a thigh bone
To use as a toothpick.
It is the hunter who has done this for me.
(Bird 1974: 3, cited in Okpewho 1992: 27)

In the tradition of praise poetry, the aim is to cement and ease social relations, just as it was for the slaves observed by Edwards and in weddings where two families are united in a social contract where a harmonious relationship is essential for the well-being of one and all. It should be remembered that the oratory which marks occasions such as weddings and engagements has its roots in a tradition extending for hundreds of years back to Africa, before the diaspora and it is against this background that it must be interpreted.

Political Speeches
The political speeches of Black orators also need to be seen in the context of their African antecedents. For example, the Ashanti linguists, professional political spokesmen of kings and chiefs among the Akan, were noted for their eloquent speech. They often had to perfect the speech of a ruler who was inarticulate (cf Finnegan 1970: 447).

The political speeches of prominent Black politicians and community activists illustrate the same forceful and dynamic delivery documented for African orators. Marcus Garvey, the Jamaican political activist, illustrates the flamboyant oratory and eloquent speech of many Black leaders. The following is an extract of the speech he delivered at the Royal Albert Hall, London June 6, 1928:

> Liberate the minds of men and ultimately you will liberate the bodies of men. And I am here tonight as a representative of the New Negro in finance, the new Negro in art, the new Negro in literature, the new Negro in music, the New Negro in economics, the new Negro in science. But the new Negro

is also thinking in terms of perpetual motion; the Negro is also thinking in terms of the hidden mysteries of the worlds; and you do not know what the oppressed and suppressed Negro, by virtue of his condition and circumstances, may give to the world as a surprise (cited in Garvey & Essien-Udom 1977: 57).

Although many political leaders tend to use a prepared lecture format there is still much improvisation. There are also many dynamic speakers who do not seem to use a written text. Most notable of these are the civil rights leaders from America, Reverend Al Sharpton and Reverend Jesse Jackson. Some political activists, especially in America, cross the sacred-secular spectrum producing speeches which sound like sermons. Mitchell (1970) goes so far as to suggest that the 'I have a Dream' speech of Dr Martin Luther King was in fact a sermon on the basis of features such as call and response (see chapter six), repetition (see chapter seven), imagery and metaphors.

In the UK context, Reverend Hughie Andrews brings the same sermon-like qualities to the political arena. Talking about the Black Supplementary School Movement in London, January 1990, for instance, he says:

What, then, are supplementary schools and what were the circumstances that led to setting them up? First we must deal with the circumstances. Black supplementary schools were born out of the womb of struggle and have since been faced with the continuing task of fighting for quality education for our children. Do you understand what I'm saying?

Audience response: Yes sir yes [laughter].

We came home to the 'mother country' believing that our children would receive a good education, but the realisation that the system was failing them made many Black parents anxious and they began to express themselves in the Black education movement towards the end of the 60's.

Audience response: hmhm, yes, tell us.

The high level of audience participation encouraged by the speech is far more reminiscent of a Pentecostal sermon than of the more self-contained White political speech.

Oratory conducted in formal settings is an essential aspect of 'sweet talk'. It ranges from sermons and testimonies, and speeches at weddings in the sacred context to official and political speeches in the secular context. The language is colourful, original and dynamic. It is used to teach moral values, impart wisdom and facilitate social harmony.

Storytelling
Storytelling is another feature of Black culture firmly rooted in the African oral tradition. It is discussed, for instance, in African settings by Finnegan (1970, 1988), Cosentino (1982) and Okpewho 1992); by Heath (1983) and Mitchell (1986) in the USA; and by Crowley (1966), Barrett (1976) andTanna (1984) in the Caribbean. Storytelling is less well documented in Britain, although Sutcliffe (1982) pays some attention to oral narrative among young Blacks.

The limitations on story tellers depend on local conventions. In some societies there are no restrictions, in others there is a definite expectation as to who should tell stories. In some areas, the women - often older women - practise this art; in others, it is the men (Finnegan 1970).

Professional storytellers are common in Africa but there is a difference in image and status between rural performers and their urban counterparts. Storytellers in rural settings may be confined to their village and consequently have to rely on other means to survive economically. In rural Nigeria, for example, Okpewho (1992) reports that storytellers such as Simayi of Ubulu-Uno have other jobs. In contrast to the rural artist, many urban storytellers perform frequently for the media, make a reasonable amount of money on a regular basis and have a comfortable life-style. Some, such as Salawa Abeni of Nigeria, are wealthy and well-respected.

Many storytellers in the Caribbean are talented individuals who learn the stories from their elders and perform simply for pleasure. However, there are also a few well-known professional storytellers. In Grenada Paul Keens-Douglas is a notable raconteur. In Jamaica, the queen of storytelling is Louise Bennett; the late Ranny Williams was also a popular performer. In Britain, professional storytellers include Faustin Charles, Grace Hallsworth and Merle Collins.

In Africa and throughout the diaspora, storytelling is one of the entertainments provided for an evening of relaxation. Stories are often performed at social gatherings in both sacred and secular contexts. They are told on the street and in the home; adults in the community often gather the young to tell Anancy stories. Indeed any social occasion could result in a story session. Ranny Williams of Jamaica, for example, recalled that he learned the art of oral narrative from his Maroon grandmother:

> We would sit down around her. Maybe in the barbecue, maybe in the kitchen at crop time while we were shelling peas and so, or maybe just sitting down there and telling us those stories. And other relatives too, old people who just would be telling us and we learned the stories in this way. We never set out to learn the stories. We just learned them from hearing them told to us. Country people were happy for any opportunity to bake and cook and so on and have a big feast and thing, and you'd be encouraged to tell an Anansi story, you know (cited in Tanna 1984: 29).

There is great similarity in plots, motifs and characters in story telling over wide expanses of time and space. One of the most common themes is the tug of war which involves the small trickster animal who outdoes the more powerful one. The small animal in question, however, differs. For example, in many parts of Central Africa he is known as the hare; in West Equatorial Africa he is a tortoise. Brer Rabbit appears in the Savannah areas of West Africa and reappears in similar stories in Black communities in the Americas; the spider found in the forest region of Ghana, the Ivory Coast and Sierra Leone corresponds directly to 'Anancy' in the Caribbean.

In Africa, America and the Caribbean there are, of course, many other stories about the ordinary and the extraordinary, some about legendary heroes or ancestors and some which recount actions of various supernatural beings. Another common theme is the explanation for behaviour seen in the world today, with reference to animals, for example, how wasp got its sting. Stories of this kind often end with a moral, sometimes in the form of a well known proverb, such as, 'strangers should be treated well' or 'it is ill advised to oppress the weak'.

One of the main functions of storytelling is to entertain. In the secular domain, young Black people take pleasure in recounting stories which centre around family exploits. The following extract from the Dudley data is one such account. The narrative by Roy is about what happened when his sister, Yvette, ate his lemon curd. He captivates the audience of friends, often attracting comments of approval and generating a great deal of laughter. He starts at a fairly moderate pace:

> I remember one time, I remember one time right, um, I'd been going to the warehouse with me, dad and that right, so sister Ferron bought me this bottle of lemon curd, so I was tecking my tongue, licking lemon curd for weeks and one time I come from, went out somewhere and when I came back, my lemon curd bottle was empty, and when I found out and I found that Yvette had done it.

At this point, the delivery increases in tempo and builds into a crescendo. His British English delivery slides rapidly into broad Patois, as he performs first the role of his tell-tale brother, then the role of his infuriated father.

> So me and Yvette had a fight, boof box her up and when he came from, when dad came from work ... dad was on six till two, that was the worse shift as well, cause daddy come from work and he goes mummy goes, 'Roy, daddy, you know what

Roy do? Him no box up Yvette inna im mout mek her mout bleed, mi ha fi go give her water fi drink'. Den they go 'come here. What me tell you bout dem girls a day time, me no tell ou fi behave you self, me no tell you fi behave you self no? Mi soon come'.

[Roy, daddy, do you know what Roy did? He hit Yvette in her mouth and made it bleed. I had to give her some water to drink. Come here Roy? What did I tell you about those girls? Did I not tell you to behave yourself? Did I not tell you to behave yourself? I'll be here in a while]

The climax comes as Roy's father delivers his punishment.

Him come back, belt fie, fie, fie, fie, right, and when im done he says he goes 'lie down a ground dere, mi soon come back'. And him call everybody inside, you know so they had to sit on me, there was a little bit left, so they had to finish off ... He said 'Roy, let me tell you someting', and den he put the bottle in front of me. 'You a go kill you sister fi food, mek me tell you someting, me a kill you first'.

The onomatopoeic chorus of 'fie, fie, fie' as Roy's father beats him with the belt is greeted with howls of mirth from members of the audience totally engrossed in the performance.

Roy exhibits the classic qualities of the good storyteller, summed up by Barrett (1976: 31) in the following terms:

What gives these Black narratives a quality and flavouring of their own, despite the fact that in a number of instances amalgamation of certain European elements is highly probable, are the special effects employed by the story-teller, which run the gamut from idiomatic language tinged by piquant speech to gesticulation and the acting out of parts against a background of manufactured noises, chants and mimicry.

Everyone in a conversation may want to recount their story. Heath (1983) explains that young story-tellers in Trackton, a Black community in America, must be aggressive in inserting their stories into an on-going stream of discourse. Consequently story-telling is highly competitive, a quality which contributes to the entertainment value. Heath (1983: 181-182) records the following story told by twelve-year-old Terry to a group of boys after his first week in a new school:

> You don't know me, but you will. I'm Terry Moore. You might think I look sissy, sittin' in dat class ackin' like I'm working you know. But I'm de tough one around here, and I done been down to Mr X. office more'n you can count. You know, I'm de onliest one what can stand up to dat paddle of his. He burn me up. I'ma tell you 'bout dat (pause).

Terry begins his story by boasting about his strength because he has been to the headmaster's office on several occasions to face the physical onslaught of the paddle or baton.

> One day I was walkin' down de hall, now you ain't 'posed to do dat, 'less 'n you got a pass, and I ain't had no pass on my ass. And all of a sudden I hear somebody comin', and dere was a feelin' like my ass was caught for sure. And it was Mr X and he come roun' de corner like he knowed I was dere. I took out runnin' (pause) now don't even run 'less'n you know you don't hafta stop. Dat was my mistake. It was good while it lasted.

He continues to give a highly detailed and exaggerated account of his adventure. He gestures dramatically, contorts his face, groans and uses other sounds to convey the story:

> I run all the way down Main, but my feet 'n legs start hurtin' and I got me a strain, but den a power like Spider Man, and I look back and dis web fall over Mr X and he struggle (pause), and he struggle (pause), and he struggle. 'n den dis big old roach (cockroach) come outta de walls of dem ol' buildings on Main, and that roach start eatin' his head (pause), his fingers (pause), 'n his toes (pause) 'n he holler, 'n

> I come to de end of Main and I stop to watch ... 'Hey Terry
> lis'n hep me' ... You gonna burn dat paddle up?' He go 'You
> can have it, you can have it. So I let 'im up, and call off dat
> roach and spider web, and we back to school... He git me, 'n
> took dat paddle to me, and to' (tore) me up (long pause). But
> somewhere out dere, old Spider Man, he know I'm takin' it
> for him, and he hep me out next time.

Terry suggests, then, that the headmaster once out of his school
and onto Main (one of the poor areas of the town) has no strength
to overcome the forces there. The roach (cockroach) attacks and
the headmaster becomes Terry's victim, pleading for help. Terry
extolls his own strength, wit and wisdom and shows he knows the
school rules:

> You have to have a pass in the school hall; don't run away
> unless you are sure you can outrun your pursuer.

He also shows that he knows implicit rules; children invariably
get caught. However, he leaves no doubt about his undaunted
spirit in spite of what may sound like defeat at the hands of the
headmaster.

Storytelling not only entertains; it also teaches. It can be used, for
instance, to put across lessons for life or to settle important
matters of dispute (Shorter 1974: 83). It can also be used to
transmit salient values and ideas, such as 'it is ill-advised to
oppress the weak'. Storytelling is also an integral element in Black
preaching style (Tomlin 1988) where the preacher uses anecdote
to illustrate important points and highlight moral issues. Stories
are sometimes biblical, at other times they are true narratives of
personal experiences; occasionally, they are stories which are
well-known. Take the following biblical story of a woman who
had internal bleeding told by Reverend Chris Tunde Joda of
Nigeria and recorded by the Voice of Faith Ministries in Lagos,
Nigeria:

Reverend Joda Mark's Gospel chapter five. Listen to this one,
              hallelujah
Congregation: amen
              response
Reverend Joda: Mark's gospel chapter five. listen to this one. I tell
              you, you get excited tonight. Listen to the story.
              That pitiable woman twelve years internal
              haemorrhage no head no tail.

The Reverend Joda continues his narrative in a humorous vein. He
improvises and relates it to contemporary society. He also
emphasises the point that there are situations which affect one's
finances.

Every physician she knew. She went to the best gynaecologist.
She went to the best of the obstetrician. She went to Lagos. She
went to London. She went to America. I mean she went
everywhere [laughs]. Bible says she spent all that she had. You
know people like that? Have you been a victim of that? Just
spending, just spending... She grew worse was the close of verse
twenty six, but look at verse twenty seven. When she had heard of
Jesus. She heard about a man of Galilee that was going about
doing good and healing.

His voice becomes progressively louder as he recounts the scene
of the ill woman as she struggles through the crowd to touch
Jesus.

She heard about that man called Jesus and I tell you something
began to happen in her life and the Bible tells me she came in the
crowd behind and touched his garment.

In traditional Black preaching style he dramatises the events by
taking on the role of the ill woman and imitating her voice. He
also uses repetition to emphasise important points.

She said - and literal Greek says - she kept on saying, she
kept on saying, she kept on saying, "hey that man is gonna be
my redeemer, that man is gonna be my Saviour. I've tried

everything I know. I've been to the doctors. I've been to the juju man (witch doctor). I've been to the native doctors, nobody's helped me yet, but I've heard about a Jesus he's gonna help me" and she kept on saying. "If I touch the hem of his garment I shall, I shall. It's not a maybe. I've got into the end of my road. If I don't touch him my story's gonna end right here but I believe something good can happen to me". And the Bible says that when she touched the hem of his garment - verse twenty nine - and straight away the fountain of her blood was dried up and she felt in her body that she was healed of that plague. Notice the Bible calls it a plague. Internal bleeding for twelve years is a plague.

As the story enfolds, the Reverend Joda expresses the underlying Christian theme that Jesus has complete control over every circumstance, including chronic illness, and is able to perform miracles against all the odds.

You carry it about in your body. It makes you an outcast in the society. You can't mix with your friends. You can't mix with your relatives. You're totally ostracised from everybody you love and what the devil intended to be a permanent shame until she died. Jesus turned the other side of the coin. She's healed. He says to her in verse thirty four daughter your faith has made you whole go in peace. She was in pieces [laughs]. Jesus said 'You've been made whole now you can be in peace and be whole of thy plague'. Hallelujah!

Reverend Joda makes a pun on the words *peace* and *pieces* to further illustrate the point that Jesus can cure all illnesses.

The power of storytelling thus lies in the ways in which it teaches through entertainment. Competent storytellers hold the audience in the palm of their hands as they excite the imagination, amuse and totally engage those privileged to participate.

Dub Poetry
Finally, we will focus on dub poetry which is a development of toasting and described by Onuora (cited in Morris 1983: 150) as

poetry that has a built in reggae rhythm. It tends to be much slower in delivery than toasting and is more like speech than singing. Often, a musical background accompanies dub poetry. It is often conducted at cultural events such as poetry and drama festivals. Well-known artists like the late Mikey Smith from Jamaica and Linton Kwesi Johnson and Jean Binta Breeze in Britain are exponents of this art form. The content of dub poetry tends to be political and unlike reggae or ragga does not contain any sexual overtones. It focuses strongly on the circumstances and oppression of Black people. It tends to encourage Black people to be more racially aware and proud of their African ancestry, as can be seen in the following excerpt of the poem performed by Martin Glyn at St Anthony's College, Oxford, in 1986:

You might want to call me European
with my background from the Caribbean
but our roots in a dispute is an African

so people I beg you
don't call me no European
don't call me a West Indian
don't call me a Black American

and don't call me no coloured man
Because our roots in a dispute is an African.

Dub poetry is a part of the verbal creativity found in Black culture. Words are especially chosen for their stylistic effect.

Conclusion
The previous chapter examined bad talk; the present chapter focuses on sweet talk. Sweet talk is respectable in content and context. It takes place both in sacred contexts, such as prayers, sermons and testimonies, and in secular contexts such as political speeches and dub poetry. Occasionally speech events such as storytelling and 'throwing words,' are found in both sacred and secular settings.

While bad talk is the domain of those with little power in society, good talk is associated with the status quo: ie, preachers, church goers and politicians. Interestingly, it performs a range of functions very similar to those of good talk: it entertains; it establishes the reputation of the performer; it provides important insights into the values of the group; it teaches. But whereas bad talk achieves its end by mocking and challenging accepted values (thereby acting as a steam valve for any anti-social impulse), good talk performs a similar role by undermining the values of the group.

CHAPTER 6

CALL AND RESPONSE

ಬಿ ಬಿ ಬಿ

The focus for the present chapter is call-response, a fundamental feature of African communication in which an audience either echoes or adds to the utterance of a performer or soloist. There is evidence of highly stylised call-response behaviour in many Black communities all over the world, including Africa, the Caribbean, America and Britain.

A great deal of the discussion has centred on call-response in sacred contexts. Writers in this area include Smitherman (1977), Niles (1985), Rosenberg (1988) and Mitchell (1970; 1990) in America, and Sutcliffe & Tomlin (1986) and Callender & Cameron in Britain (1990). However, increasing attention, has also been given in the North American literature to the use of call-response in secular contexts. Writers such as Abrahams (1976), Erickson (1984) and Kochman (1981) have written extensively on this area.

Call-response is symptomatic of the highly interactive nature of Black speech events. Speaking of the difference between Black and White speech patterns in America, Abrahams (1976:9), for instance, asserts that:

> The psychic distance of the European-American
> performance system is regarded as coldness by
> Blacks; rather they expect a high degree of

complementary audience participation in
answer to their efforts...The Black performer
[in contrast] does not try to astound the audiences so much
as get them 'into it', setting up conventional
rhythms that will elicit the vital response from
the audience.

In a similar vein, Smitherman (1977:108) argues that the use of
call-response reflects the traditional African world view inherited
by Blacks in the diaspora, according to which the universe is
rhythmic in nature and seen as composed of natural and
supernatural forces which are both interactive and interdependent
(cf Mbiti 1977). All individuals are expected to actively
participate in speech events. As Thompson (1974: 28) points out,
"call and response ... far from constituting matters of structure, are
in actuality levels of perfected social interaction".

In call-response, the audience responds to the performer, who, in
turn, shapes his or her performance according to the audience
response. A favourable response will encourage the performer to
continue in the same or similar vein; a muted response may
suggest a change of course or new strategies. The interaction of
audience and performer is thus a highly sensitive one; this is
indeed a symbiotic relationship. Such a symbiotic relationship
depends to a large degree on shared experiences and group
solidarity.

The purpose of the present chapter is to explore various forms and
functions of call-response in sacred and in secular settings and to
document this more fully in a wide variety of Black communities
in Africa, the Caribbean, America and, particularly, in Britain.

Forms of Call and Response
An analysis of call-response in many different settings
demonstrates that this phenomenon can take a variety of forms.
Perhaps the most useful discussion to date is provided by
Smitherman (1977: 107) who identifies five different kinds of
response: co-signing, on T, encourager, repetition, and completer
statements. Smitherman draws primarily on African-American

data in sacred contexts. It is possible to apply her analysis, however, to a much wider range of contexts and to data from a variety of Black speech communities; and to extend this analysis to include phenomena such as co-narration and individual call-response.

A discussion of the forms of call and response needs to take into account the prosodic and paralinguistic devices which are used to cue audience involvement in both speech and music; it also needs to examine the closely related phenomenon of overlapping which often co-occurs with call-response behaviour.

Co-Signing

The most common type of response, co-signing, indicates agreement with the speaker's point. It is often realised in the sacred realm as 'Yes', 'Amen', 'Praise him', 'Tell it' and 'Hallelujah', and, in secular contexts, as 'hmhm', 'Yes my dear', 'Yeah' or, among Black British youth, 'Innit'. It can also take the form of a woofing noise made after the artist has completed a performance.Take the following example of co-signing in a British church context where Pastor Peterking's delivery is echoed with appropriate responses from the congregation:

Pastor Peterking (call):   You know it takes a person with good
                           memory to give God thanks.
Congregation (response): Praise the Lord.
Pastor Peterking (call):   There is a tendency in man to forget.
Congregation (response): Praise him.
Pastor Peterking (call):   But God never forgets.
Congregation (response): Amen.
Pastor Peterking (call):   Remember when God healed the man
                           with leprosy, do you remember?
Congregation (response): Yes, oh hallelujah.

The responses from the congregation serve to show approval for the Pastor; they offer him feedback on his performance.

There is also a high degree of co-signing in informal conversations. In an extract from the Dudley data, Roy discusses his use of Patois and English when speaking to a Black person. His observations or 'calls' are regularly punctuated with the appropriate responses from Elvis:

Roy (call):	If I go down the road now and met a Black person for the first time, if they speak Patois I think I'd speak back in Patois. I think when he's using English.
Elvis (response):	Yeah.
Roy (call):	I'd speak back, if he was a Black person, I'd speak in English back to them.
Elvis (response):	Yeah, yeah that's right yeah
Roy (call):	I change the way I speak to suit the person.
Elvis (response):	Yeah, yeah you do.

Elvis' responses do not add new information, they simply signal approval to Roy who feels free to continue holding the floor with the current topic of conversation.

On T

Closely related to co-signing is what Smitherman (1977: 107) describes as on-T, an extremely powerful co-signing response acknowledging that something the speaker has just said is 'dead on time'. On-T can take the form of both verbal responses such as 'Yassuh!' and paralinguistic and non-verbal ones, including clapping hands, stamping feet and jumping. In America, for example, phrases such as 'Who you telling?' 'Shonuff' and 'Gone wit yo bad self' are used to signal enthusiastic verbal responses of this kind; in Sierra Leone it is indicated by terms such as 'Woi' (fancy that); in Jamaica, we find 'En ma/sa!' and, in Britain, terms like 'Whaat', 'Go dea!' or 'You know!' After the preacher or singer has completed a performance, a specific movement, in which the hand is raised to head level and then lowered in a pointing movement, is used by the audience to show whole-hearted approval.

Take the following example, from Smitherman (1977: 105), of a conversation among a group of African-American women at a beauty parlour about the relative importance of Black and White people.

Female (caller):   You know, a whitey ain shit,
                              now this--
Female responders):   Who you tellin
(all at once):   Nigger ain shit, either, doan put
                              it all on the white man. Hey
                              uhm hip to it! Amen, girl, gon,
                              talk bout it!

The responses, 'Hey uhm hip to it!' or 'gon, talk bout it!' emphasise whole- hearted agreement with the statement that both White and Black people are the same: neither have little value when compared with 'shit'. The caller has hit a note with the responders; she has spoken directly to their experience, as indicated by these on-T responses.

Encouraging

Encouraging, the third form of response identified by Smitherman, is used to urge a speaker to continue in the vein in which they started: 'It's what you saying?' 'A true?' 'No?' (meaning 'yes?') 'You lie?' (meaning, 'Is that the truth?'). In Black preaching this device is used regularly to demonstrate rapport with the preacher. In West African charismatic and Pentecostal churches, for example, the audience say 'Hallelujah' to encourage the preacher. In the African-American Pentecostal and Baptist churches, members of the congregation who use encouraging interjections such as 'Glory to God', or 'Take you time preacher' are referred to as being in the "Amen Corner" (cf Spillers 1971: 19). 'Glory', 'Glory to God', 'Preach it preacher', 'Truly', 'Yes', 'Hmhm', 'Come on now preacher', 'Bless him Lord', 'Yea Lord' are some of the encouraging responses known as "bearing up the preacher" given by congregations identified in a Black British context by Tomlin (1988). Take the following example, from a church in Dudley where Pastor Peterking urges the congregation to involve God in future plans:

Pastor Peterking (call):	Whenever we are planning make sure God is in it.
Congregation (response):	Yes sir, tell us.
Pastor Peterking (call):	Don't try to jump in front of God..
Congregation (response):	No, no, bless him Lord.
Pastor Peter King (call):	And don't follow too far behind.
Congregation (response):	Come on now Preacher.

The preacher is spurred on in his delivery by the constant encouraging comments. The intensity of the audience's response signals to the preacher that his points have been well-received. As Rosenberg (1988: 65) points out, 'When an audience is responsive the preacher catches its enthusiasm'.

In secular contexts, encouraging responses are equally important and are often used at key moments in the performance. During storytelling sessions among the Limba of Sierra Leone, for instance, a person known as an answerer shouts words like 'Ndo' (yes), and 'Ee' (really) at appropriate points in the story to encourage the storyteller (cf Finnegan 1967: 67).

Encouraging responses are also used, of course, in informal conversations. In the following example from the Dudley data, Kevin recounts to Sammy the problems he had setting up the amplifiers at a party he was organising:

Kevin (call):	Mi have to run down and sen somebody down at your yard for di amplifier.
Sammy (response):	Bwoy, yeah.
Kevin (call):	An den after dat stop ... set back up again.
Sammy (response):	A no lie?

Kevin (call):	Dat was a disaster
Sammy (response):	No?
Kevin (call):	Saturday was very hard work
	the party nearly mash up.
Sammy (response):	What?

Sammy shows support for Kevin, encouraging him to elaborate on the theme. In this instance, *bwoy, yeah* and *a no lie?* (literally meaning 'Is it a lie'?) are used to urge the speaker to continue in the same vein.

Repetition
A fourth kind of response involves the repetition or partial repetition of the main speaker's call. Take for example, the following informal conversation between two Black British students:

Sandra (call):	I don't know where she is going
	with herself.
Jackie (response):	Yes I don't know where she's
	going my dear
Sandra (call):	You see how she stays.
Jackie (response):	I see her my dear.

This kind of call-response behaviour is equally evident in the sacred context. Take the following appeal from Pastor Peterking to his Dudley congregation to be sincere Christians and not to indulge in vices which could adversely affect their eternal destiny. Note the repetition of *blame* and *so sad.*

Pastor Peterking (call):	Sometimes we get weak.
	What do we do? *Blame*
	others.
Congregation (response):	*Blame yourself*, Yes
	Praise him.
Pastor Peterking (call):	It will be a sad cry for the
	drunkard and the smoker
	this morning that is in the
	street.

Congregation (response):	Hmhmh Yes, Preach it Sir.
Pastor Peterking (call):	Both of us to meet up at the same place.
Congregation (response):	My God.
Pastor Peterking (call):	It will be *so sad.*
Congregation (response):	*So sad, so sad.*

Often preachers will explicitly instruct the congregation to repeat the exact words uttered so as to engage them with the topic of the sermon. For example, a Birmingham preacher from an Apostolic Church offered this performance:

Preacher (call):	Say, *Fresh oil'*
Congregation (response):	*Fresh oil.*
Preacher (Call):	*Fresh oil.*
Congregation (response):	*Fresh oil.*

In this instance, the preacher is relying on group knowledge and underlying values. The word *fresh* can be used in Black speech for anything that is pure. In Pentecostalism, oil is a symbol of spiritual sustenance. The repetition of *fresh oil* signals clearly to the congregation that this will be the focus for the sermon.

Political speakers use this same device in a secular context. In the 1984 Presidential campaign, for instance, Jesse Jackson engaged in a call-response sequence in which the audience were specifically invited to repeat his words. The calls and responses grow progressively louder until they reach a dramatic climax:

Jackson (call):	I am (fairly loud)
Audience (response):	I am (fairly loud)
Jackson (call):	Somebody (fairly loud)
Audience (response):	Somebody (fairly loud)
Jackson (call):	I am (fairly loud)
Audience (response):	I am (fairly loud)
Jackson (call):	Somebody (louder)
Audience (response):	Somebody (louder)
Jackson (call):	I am (louder)

Audience (response):	I am (louder)
Jackson (call):	Somebody (very loud)
Audience (response):	Somebody (very loud)
Jackson (call):	Somebody (very loud)
Audience (response):	Somebody (very loud).

The use of repetition in call-response sequences is clearly a very valuable way to reinforce a point. Repetition is, of course, by no means restricted to call-response behaviour. It takes a wide variety of forms and serves an equally wide range of functions which will be explored in greater depth in chapter seven.

Completer Statements

The final category of response identified by Smitherman concerns comments which complete the statement of the main speaker. Sometimes they occur in response to a request from the speaker; sometimes they occur spontaneously. This is a particularly common device in the sacred realm where well known songs, choruses and biblical verses form a valuable knowledge base which can be drawn upon in call-response behaviour. In the following example from a Dudley church, Pastor Peterking makes reference to the omnipotence of God by using the words of a familiar chorus. The congregation completes his utterance, drawing on the same chorus:

Pastor Peterking (call):	But don't God know us?
Congregation (response):	Yes sar, yes.
Pastor Peterking (call):	What do we sing sometimes? 'Whether we are wrong...'
Congregation (response):	' or whether we are right , He knows'.

The group usually responds in unison and both the speaker and audience are part of one organic whole.

Smitherman provides a useful framework for discussion of call and response by offering the categories exemplified above. Such a framework should not, of course, be used to reduce highly dynamic verbal behaviour to an over simplistic or unduly static description. It can be argued, for instance, that there is considerable leakage between co-signing, on -T and encouraging exchanges. It is also the case that some sequences can be described in terms of more than one category. In an African-American context, Erikson (1984: 140), for instance, cites a discussion of voting fraud in a local election campaign. The dominant speaker, Jim, seeks support and validation from the other participants who oblige by repeating his call, *'ain't sposed to'*.

Jim:	That's all they _____ because once they get behind the curtains, see ... *ain't nobody sposed to* mess with, *ain't nobody sposed to* be back there with them..
Ed:	No they *ain't sposed* to be back there.
Joe:	They ain't.
Al:	They ain't.
Jim:	Sposed to but they do *ain't sposed* to be there but they do.

This sequence illustrates both repetition of t*hey ain't sposed to* and *they ain't* by Ed, Joe and Al and a completion statement by Jim.

It is also helpful to consider at this point two further aspects of call-response which fall outside the framework given by Smitherman: co-narration and individual call-response.

Co-Narration
Co-narration is a phenomenon closely related to call-response whereby speakers complete each other's statements, often alternating rapidly. In this case, however, co-narrators are developing a theme, rather than completing a well-known formula.

Clark (1977, cited in Okpewho 1992: 62) illustrates the co-narrative style of the traditional African oral performance. In his recordings of the remarkable exploits of Ozidi and his witch grandmother, Oreame, members of the audience co-narrate a passage that describes the old witch Oreame transformed into a young woman:

Narrator:	Indeed with those breasts ...
Audience 1:	She was like a young woman.
Audience 2:	A young woman.
Narrator:	If you saw her Lagos blouse, or her headtie, you'd seen a spectacle! ...
Audience 1:	Most graceful.
Audience 2:	And charming.

Interestingly, co-narration is also a part of African-American repertoire. Erickson (1984: 136-137), for instance, reports on the co-narrative style of Jim and Ed, the same African-American adolescents, in the example above, in a conversation which highlights the contradictions surrounding age and legal rights and obligations:

Jim:	When the cop come in there they put the man in ail plus get us
Ed:	'N' put us in there too and everybody that was in that tavern
Jim:	So we couldn't sing ... yet and still you can go get in the army.

The same phenomenon is regularly found in the Dudley data. Marcia and Pauline, for instance, co-narrate their mother's desire to wear the type of clothes worn in Jamaica where there is tremendous propriety among Christian women:

Marcia:	My mum now ... she's old fashioned. She'd like to dress like when she's back in Jamaica umm de dress mus
Pauline:	Jus reach de floor
Marcia:	She say it too short
Pauline:	It too short, so it afi ketch over im knee down here so.

Individual Call-response

As we have seen, call-response usually takes the form of the main speaker or performer calling for audience participation. It can also take the form of individual performers calling and responding to themselves. The popular African-American artist Stevie Wonder, for example, plays many instruments, calling and responding to himself, the instrument and the listener (Smitherman 1977: 113). Solo or lead singers also call and respond to themselves. Take the following song by Margaret Singana from the African group Ipi 'N Tombia:

Call:	Memories me, that once I lived, I was alive and now I only survive. I a ho.
Response:	But where is my place?
Call:	I a ho.
Response:	I smile but is this my face.
Call:	I a ho.
Response:	I cry but where are the tears?
Call:	I a ho.
Response:	I die the death of no fears.

In a similar vein, the sermon by the African-American preacher, Reverend D McDowell of Bakersfield, contains several lines from spirituals where the preacher is calling and responding to himself:

Call:	God is our refuge. And strength. Am well-proved helpmate in trouble.
Response:	I'm in trouble this evenin.' Yes I am. I said I'm in trouble this evenin.'

(cited in Rosenberg 1988: 22)

The Performer's Cues
The audience often responds spontaneously to the performer's call. However, there are also occasions when the performer is more directive and specifically asks for the audience's response.(cf Niles 1985). The calls which are used in this way are normally well-known and widely used. In almost all African cultures, for instance, the permission of the audience to begin a narrative performance is invoked by the use of a set formula such as the following Hausa example:

Narrator (call):   Gata nan gata nan ku (Here's a story for you)

Audience (response):   Ta so mu ju ta (It come we hear it - let us hear it).

(Dalphinis 1985: 182)

Similarly, in Bahamian folklore, the word 'Bunday' is used by the narrative performer to test whether or not the crowd wants to hear the story, as a means of getting the audience's attention so the story can be told, during and at the end of a storytelling performance (Crowley 1966).

Other calls related to particular contexts include, 'Will somebody help me?' used by Blues singers at the end of a musical phrase, or, 'Is there anybody in the house?' used by rappers. In a sacred context the preacher intersperses his sermon with, 'Let the Church say amen', 'Will somebody help me?' 'Can I have a witness?' (Can someone affirm what I am saying?) or 'Hello?' (Can I have a response?) - a phrase used by West Africans, African-American, Caribbean and Black British preachers. By the same token, a person who offers a testimony will begin with, 'Shall we praise the Lord?' Performers also use non-verbal signals to elicit a response from the audience. For instance, preachers sometimes jump up and down while singers walk towards the audience.

Tonal Semantics
In situations where audience and performer do not rely on shared knowledge of this kind, the performer uses a range of other devices to cue responses which Smitherman (1977: 134) calls 'tonal semantics'. This term:

> Refers to the use of voice rhythm and vocal inflection to convey meaning ... In using the semantics of tone, the voice is employed like a musical instrument with improvisations, riffs, and all kinds of playing between the notes. This rhythmic pattern becomes a kind of acoustical phonetic

alphabet and gives black speech its songified or musical quality.

Distinctive Black prosody is particularly evident in, although not confined to, sacred settings. It is often manifested in rhythmic speech Take the sermon of Reverend ChrisTunde Joda of Nigeria, for example:

> Pastor Joda (call): God should be a God you can pray to and he can answer your prayer. He should be a God that you can talk to in the morning, talk to in the afternoon, talk to in the midnight hour and he can be as real to you as any other time, hallelujah.
> Congregation (response): hallelujah.

Often exaggerated stress is placed either at regular intervals or on key words in a performance, in this case *talk to* . Similarly, take the following extract from a powerful sermon entitled God is a Jealous God delivered by Pastor Ulrich Rolle, from Antigua:

> Pastor Rolle (call): He is saying you ought to be mine. You ought to be mine exclusively.
> Congregation (response): Amen, praise the Lord.
> Pastor Rolle (call): You see when God separates a nation or life unto Himself. It ought to be mine and nobody else. It ought to be mine wholly It ought to be mine truly t ought to be mine completely Because I am a jealous God.

Pastor Rolle places exaggerated stress at regular intervals throughout the first call and the words which follow in the second call. The exaggerated stress, in combination with the very loud delivery, ensure that the congregation become emotionally involved in the sermon. Note, incidentally, the use of words such as *Himself* and *else* and *wholly, truly* and *completely* to create rhythm and cadence.

Testimonies, also make use of rhythmic speech. Take the testimony of Sister Smith from a church in Dudley:

Call: I'm right down glad I've ever been to Jesus I'm right down glad my heart is free. Response: Praise the Lord! Hallelujah!
Call: I'm going to conquer Satan and I have no time to tarry. The Bible says if my mother won't come, If anyone won't come, I won't let him hinder me.
Response: Amen
Call: For I'm on my way to heaven and it's my desire to see the King.
Response: Praise the Lord.

As was the case for Pastor Rolle, Sister Smith gives exaggerated stress at regular intervals throughout her testimony.

Preachers often use deliberately slow and exaggerated pronunciation of important words. Rather than saying 'God', for instance, they will say [   ] aspirating the final consonant. They also make use of elongated articulation of single words, heavy breathing and lengthy pauses between words and phrases. In the extract from the sermon by Pastor Rolle cited above, for example, the climax is punctuated by dramatic inhalations that sound almost like groans. 'Talk-singing,' of this kind is often signals the climax of the sermon and arouses appropriate responses from the congregation. Below is a short extract of a sermon from the Jamaican, Pastor Blair, delivered at the Youth and Christian education Convention in April 1990 at De Montfort Hall, Leicester, which illustrates this phenomenon:

Pastor Blair: I'm telling you tonight Jesus is the answer.
Congregation: Jesus
Pastor Blair: He's the Rose of Sharon, the lily of the
(talk singing)   valley
Congregation: Jesus
Pastor Blair: The bread when I'm hungry, my water when I'm
(talk singing) thirsty
Congregation: Yes, yeah, Jesus, hallelujah, praise the Lord

Pastor Blair:	*Jee-sus Jee-sus halleluuuuujah..* He's the aanswer. Help me preach somebody? He was both God and man. As a man he was tired and went to sleep but as God he neither slumber nor sleep. As man he was hungry but as God he took five loaves and two fishes and fed 5,000 men.
Congregation:	Jesus, Jesus, hallelujah, amen
Pastor Blair:	*Woooo, woooo, yeah ... yeah ... ahah* (intoned).

The highly dramatic effects of talk-singing demand a response from the congregation of a similar intensity; this form of tonal semantics is a potent cueing device used in the orchestration of a powerful climax.

Tonal semantics are not just confined to the sacred domain. The oratory of Dr Martin Luther King, Reverend Jesse Jackson and Malcolm X are obvious examples of political discourse which make use of distinctively Black prosody. As Spillers (1971: 19) states:

> This process, spontaneous in its thrust, is highly technical and consistent; the speaker, with his innate sense of timing and rhythm, knows exactly which words will be prominent and what phrases an audience will respond to because he has seen the technique work for his elders time and again.

On some occasions, the distinctively Black prosodies used to cue audience participation are also echoed in the responses. In King's Montgomery speech (Spillers 1971: 19), for instance, an unidentified man responded to King's rhythm by repeating the key words, 'Yessuh, we're on the move'. Subsequently, other members of the audience picked up on his lead responding to King's statements with 'We're on the move'.

There are also examples of call and response which have become popular slogans. For instance, the Black Civil Rights Movement of the 1960s, saw the emergence of the rhythmic slogan 'No pain, no gain' in which the regular beat was further emphasised by the rhyme. The main speaker(s) would chant 'No pain' while the audience responded with, 'No gain'.

Call-Response in Music and Singing

Given the highly musical qualities of much call-response behaviour in both sacred and secular speech events, it is not at all surprising to find that call-response is also a recurrent feature of Black music. Holloway (1991: 193) writes that:

> The call-response structure is the key mechanism that allows for the manipulation of time, text and pitch. The response or repetitive chorus provides a stable foundation for the improvised lines of the soloist. The use of call-response structures to generate musical change has been described many times in black music literature.

Call-response is present not only in the singing style of Black music, but also in the music itself. As far back as 1952 Waterman identified a number of ways in which African music differed from the European tradition. These included features such as polymeter, off-beat phrasing of melodic accents and, significantly for the purposes of the present discussion, overlapping call and response patterns. Take the following song from Nigeria, recorded by Okpewho (1992: 44):

Lead (call):	Mm, let's go the palace, Oh ...
Chorus (response):	Let's go to the palace
Lead (response):	Nwadobe, my son
Chorus (call):	Let's go to the palace
Lead (call):	Just look at you .

The Negro-Spirituals and African-American gospel singing, for instance, rely heavily on African musical patterns of call-response as can be seen in the well known *Swing Low, Swing Chariot:*

Lead (call):	Swing Low
Background (response):	Swing Low
Lead (call):	Swing Chariot
Background (response):	Coming for to carry me home.

Call-response is also a feature of British Black music. Black sacred and secular music in Britain is greatly influenced by a number of styles including Soca, Calypso, reggae and ragga from the Caribbean and the Blues, Soul, Jazz, and Rapping from America. As the Reverend Bazil Mead points out:

> If you go to a church in Dalston where a lot of people come from Montserrat and Barbados, you'll hear a definite calypso feel to the way they sing. Another Church will have ska or reggae beat".

(cited in Broughton 1985: 157).

However, irrespective of the style, the call-response tradition permeates British Black music. Take the following chorus of the song *My woman* by the Black British rap group, Force:

Lead (call):   You're my woman and you know I love you
Background (response): You're my woman
Lead (call):   I'm chilling out on the mountainside
Background (response): Chilling out on the mountain
Lead (call):   Love you today just the same way
Background (response): You know I love you

As Jamaicans are the dominant group in Black Pentecostal Churches, the reggae music which they transported from Jamaica to Britain merits special consideration in relation to call-response. Reggae is characterised by antiphonal call-response chanting and the repetition of short single musical phrases . *Moving up the King's High Way*, for instance, is a Gospel chorus sung to a reggae rhythm. Note the repetition of the call not only by the background singers, but by the lead singer who first introduced the call:

Lead singers (call):   Don't you know that I'm moving up the King's high way
Background (response): Up the King's high
Lead singers (response):Moving up the King's high way

Lead singers (call):	Don't you know that I'm trusting in amazing grace
Background (response):	In a amazing
Lead singers (response):	Trusting in amazing grace
Lead singers (call):	Don't you know that Satan is on my back
	Lead & Background(response): And I'll never, ever, ever turn back
Lead singers (call):	For I'm moving up, moving up, moving up Oh Lord
Background (response):	Moving up the King's highway.

Responses are not always, however, repetitions or near repetitions. Take the song *Don't Turn Around* by the Black British artists Aswan in which the response by the backing singers is quite different from the call of the lead singer:

Lead singer (call):	But don't turn around,
Background (response):	Cause you gonna see my heartbreaking
Lead singer (call):	Don't turn around
Background (response):	I don't want you to see me crying
Lead singer (call):	Just walk away
Background (response):	It's tearing me apart now your leaving.

Overlapping

The discussion to date has focused on the range of devices used by the performer to cue the audience response. Sometimes there is a smooth transition from call to response; on most occasions, however, there is a high degree of overlapping. Various writers discuss this phenomenon in Black discourse. Reisman (1974), for example, refers to this highly interactive style as contrapuntal. The counterpoint involves speaker-audience alternation, overlap between simultaneous speakers, and repetition by the same speaker, both for rhetorical emphasis and as a way of being heard. As Reisman (1974: 115) explains:

> The start of a new voice is not in itself a signal for the voice speaking to stop or to institute a process which will decide who is to have the floor.

Reisman's observations relate to Antiguan conversation. There is every reason to suppose, however, that overlapping is a much broader Black phenomenon. Kochman (1981), for instance, suggests in a discussion of African-American turn-taking that the general rule is 'interrupt when you can'. Similar speech patterns were found in the Dudley data. Take the following discussion which centres around the degree of prejudice among teachers in two local secondary school:

Terry: How de teachers dere did prejudice
Roy: I don't know Par. I don't know say of them were
Elvis: Park
Roy: Prejudiced, but some a them were prejudice
Terry: Park School
Roy: Some a dem yea Park
Terry: I tink Park School teachers was just
Roy: I didn't Trusky
Terry: Was a waste of time
Roy: Trusky was I reckon there, there are one or two of them.

Overlapping can also be found in sermons, testimonies and prayers. It tends to be more structured, however, in sacred settings than in informal secular conversations. According to Rosenberg (1988: 59), the antiphonal nature of Black sermons invites audience participation. This observation applies equally to Black Pentecostal congregations in Britain where examples of overlapping such as the following are a frequent occurrence:

Pastor Jackson (call):   Woe unto them that
Congregation (response): ... that stay at ease in Zion.

Whereas previous examples of call-response have included completer statements, in this instance, the congregation not only complete Pastor Jackson's call, but successfully anticipate his words, and respond by overlapping his call before he even has the opportunity to pause and signal that he awaits completion. Overlapping of this kind requires a very high degree of shared knowledge.

Overlapping takes on a rather different form in testimonies. The moderator, who leads the testimonial part of the service, calls upon the congregation to 'stand and testify'. In response to this request, it is not unknown for two or three enthusiastic members to testify at the same time. This mainly occurs in large meetings such as conventions, where the level of emotional intensity is very high.

Prayer can be sequential. It can also involve two or more individuals praying at the same time or overlapping. Whereas in most White contexts, when the whole congregation prays, they will be uniting in the same prayer, (for example, the Lord's Prayer), in Black Pentecostal settings it is a regular occurrence for all members of the congregation to engage in loud extemporised prayer individually and at the same time (cf Sutcliffe & Tomlin 1986).

As was the case for other aspects of call-response, overlapping is not restricted to speech, but is also a feature of music. Both rappers (MCs) and DJs, for example, rely on overlapping in their performances. The DJ art of mixing, which requires a combination of records simultaneously playing to create one song, is possibly a new manifestation of the same underlying phenomenon.

Conclusion

Call-response, then, is the Black communication patterns whereby the audience either repeats or adds to the utterance of a performer. It takes a variety of forms including co-signing, On T, encouraging, repetition and completer statements. These categories form a useful framework for discussion. However, they should not be viewed as totally discrete, since there is some degree of overlap between them. Call-response can also take the form of co-narration where speakers complete each other's statement or individual call-response in which performers both call and respond to themselves.

Often the performer makes use of shared knowledge to cue the audience. In these instances, there is heavy reliance on features such as opening and closing formulae. On other occasions tonal semantics, or distinctively Black prosody, is used as cue for audience response. Call-response also permeates Black musical traditions. Both singing and music are highly antiphonal. As well as the more structured call-response devices there is also a great deal of overlapping between speakers.

The level of co-operation and the shared responsibility for performance indicate the tremendously interactive nature of Black speech events, all of which is underpinned by a shared core of cultural knowledge and expectations. All of these features of call-response are, of course, common throughout the diaspora, in speech and music and in sacred and secular settings.

CHAPTER 7

REPETITION

ȣ ȣ ȣ

In the previous chapter, the discussion of call-response inevitably entailed some reference to the significance of repetition in Black speech events. Repetition, is however, by no means restricted to call-response behaviour. It is a phenomenon which permeates many kinds of Black performance and will form the focus for the present chapter, which will explore both its forms and its functions.

In predominantly literate societies, specific words and phrases are repeated only for limited and designed effect. The use of this stylistic device tends to be far more widespread in societies where prime importance is attached to the spoken word. The meaning attached to repetition in oral and literate contexts is also very different. Edwards & Sienkewicz (1990: 144), for instance, make this point by comparing the sonnet with a sermon by a Black preacher:

> In the sonnet, nothing can be redundant or aggregate. In the sermon and other forms of oral art, repeatable forms like formulae, proverbs and riddles form an essential part of the communal basket of threads from which the performance is woven. Thus the structural unity of the written word is analytic and creates unity by trimming the excess and the irrelevant, while in the oral world structural unity is

essentially synthetic, a constant elaboration of elements added to the fibre of the web of words.

This much more prevalent use of repetition receives comment from a number of authors (cf Rosenberg 1988; Tannen 1989). In particular, Abrahams (1976: 20-21) points to the way in which:

> This stylistic trait extends beyond the word or phrase unit into large units of speaking activity; for instance, the punch line of a joke may be repeated three or four times, if the joke has been well-received, each time eliciting laughter. Or a song or rhyme in a cant fable may be performed over and over by the narrator or, more commonly in the West Indies, by the entire group. Nor is the repetition restricted to the spoken word.

With reference to music, Lomax (1970: 191-201) describes the use of repetition as part of the common stylistic base of Black singing in Africa, Black communities in Columbia, Venezuela, America and many Caribbean islands.

The present chapter will look at repetition in a variety of Black speech contexts ranging from Africa to the Caribbean, and from America to Britain. The examples will be taken from a number of domains, sacred and secular, including informal conversation, political speeches, sermons and song. Attention will be paid first to the different forms of repetition and then to the various functions which it serves.

Forms of Repetition
Repetition can be used to achieve a number of different effects. It also takes a variety of forms, including reduplication, simple repetition, near repetition and thematic repetition. The repetition can vary in length from single words to much lengthier units such as the refrains of epics or cant fables, or proverbs and riddles.

Reduplication
Reduplication is a feature of many West African languages and creoles which has attracted frequent comment (cf Bailey 1966;

Barrett 1976; Edwards 1979; Todd 1984). It is a productive process in language, whereby words are repeated to form a compound with a variety of meanings. In Jamaican Creole, for instance, it can be used for emphasis as in *no-no* (definitely not); continual habitual action as in *cry-cry* (always crying); abundance as in *huoli-huoli* (having many holes or, in the sacred realm, sanctimonious); iteration as in *knock-knock* (to keep on knocking); attribution as in *redi-redi* (reddish); distribution as in *little-little* (a little here; a little there); and for plural reference as in *was-was* (wasps).

The use of reduplication is widespread in Jamaican and British Black speech, and is particularly marked in music. The reggae song, *Girlie, Girlie* by Sophia George provides many such examples:

Young man you too *girlie-girlie*,
You jus a flash it roun de worle,
Young man you too *girlie-girlie*,
You jus a flash it roun de worle.
Him have one a go a school,
One gwan *fool-fool.*
Im have one every time me say she tink a she rule,
One she a nurse, she say a she come first.
The other night dem going out, dem pick her new purse.
One a sell spa,
One work in a bar,
A she can smile when de two dem spar,
One *geti-geti*
One *freti-freti*
An him no have no other one but Betty.

Men are chastised for their excessive liking of women - 'Young man, you too girlie-girlie'. Women, in turn, are described as *fool-fool* (foolish), *geti-geti* (opportunist), *freti-freti* (anxious) and *flighty-flighty* (fickle).

Simple Repetition

Reduplication involves the formation of compound verbs, nouns or adjectives. Another feature of Black language is what we might label 'simple repetition', the repetition of a single word, a phrase or even an entire sentence to achieve a variety of effects from emphasis to drama. An interesting example of the simple repetition of a single word is to be found in the dialogue of *The Rag Doll*, a novel written by the Jamaican writer, Hazel Dorothy Campbell. One of the principal characters, a Christian woman called Sister Dessie, was visiting a maternity hospital as part of her ministry when she encountered a woman berating the father of her baby. Note the repetition of 'baby-fader', the Jamaican Creole and Black British term for the father of an illegitimate child:

> What fi do wid de baby? How im gwaine get food? Baby-fader disappear when him hear me sey me expecting. Never even get clothes fi it. Baby-fader sey a no fi him ... How wi gwine manage? Baby-fader no want the family planning (Campbell 1978: 15).

As was the case for reduplication, the most dramatic use of the simple repetition of a single word is to be found in music. Take for instance the use of 'wonderful' in the song of the same name performed by the British Black Merybell choir. The refrain consists quite simply of:

> Wonderful, wonderful,
> Wonderful, wonderful,
> Wonderful,
> Wonderful, wonderful,
> Wonderful.

By the same token, a phrase can be repeated to achieve a number of stylistic effects. Take the use of *im chat* in an informal conversation where the speaker was referring to someone with a reputation for gossip: "im chat, im chat, im chat, im chat, im chat so till". In a more formal context, note the use of God's will in the testimony of a deacon in a Dudley church:

It is God's will that we should be here tonight, God's will that we should be in the family, God's will that you should be adopted in him, and this was before the foundation of the world.

Simple repetition of an entire sentence is also a common feature of Black performance in a variety of contexts. Take the famous song, "No woman no cry", by the late Jamaican reggae artist, Bob Marley. The song centres around the problems and difficulties experienced by a woman who is exhorted not to cry:

Lead:	No woman no cry
Background:	No woman no cry
Lead:	No woman no cry
Background:	No woman no cry

This same kind of simple repetition was used by Jesse Jackson as a ploy to warm up his audience at the Hackney Empire in London 1990 as he started to deliver his political message.

Keep hope alive!
Keep hope alive!
Keep hope alive!
Keep hope alive!

It should be pointed out, however, that simple repetition is seldom restricted to words or phrases or sentences. Most often, speakers weave different layers of repetition into their performance as, for instance, in the case in the West African chorus, 'Higher, Higher'.

Cast your burdens unto Jesus for he cares for you, Cast your burdens unto Jesus for he cares for you.
Higher, higher, higher, higher, higher, higher, higher, higher,
Lift up Jesus higher.
Lower, lower, lower, lower, Satan, lower,
Lower, lower, lower, Satan, lower.

Here we find not only the repetition of single words like *higher* and *lower*, but of a whole sentence as in *Cast your burdens unto Jesus for he cares for you.*

Near Repetition

Closely related to simple repetition is a stylistic device labelled 'elegant variation' by Callender and Cameron (1990: 19). In this case we are dealing not with the simple repetition of a word, phrase or sentence, but with a near repetition or a paraphrase. Elegant variation is often used by speakers or performers to acknowledge the presence of the audience by paying a courteous salute.

In the sacred context, speakers will often prefix their testimony with "Greetings to my pastor: Greetings to the saints and visiting friends". This type of repetition is also illustrated in the following extract from a sermon by Jerry H Lockett, cited in Rosenberg (1988: 47).

I'm talkin' about Jesus
I'm talkin' about Jesus
I'm talkin' about the one who brought us a mighty long ways
We seen a child way up in Jerusalem
Seen Him up there settin' down amongst the doctors
Seen Him up there among the lawyers
Settin' up there among highly educated people.

Here we see the alternation or 'elegant variation' between *Jesus* and *the one*, between *a child* and *Him*, between *settin' down among*, and *settin' up among* and *there among* and *settin' up there among.*

Lists

Lists are repetitive structures which allow the speaker to develop a point. We are dealing here with the repetition not of the same word but of the same grammatical structures. Take for instance, the list of God's attributes outlined by the famous Nigerian preacher, Dr Idahosa, in a sermon at Kensington Temple, a Pentecostal church in London:

God is omnipotent
God is omnipresent.
God is on sign.
God is a God that is more than enough.

Lists can often be used as a signal for audience response. In a mainstream British context, Atkinson (1984: 49-83) uses examples from the 1983 Tory campaign to put forward the view that the competent orator will indicate appropriate points for audience response by using such rhetorical devices as three-part lists. It is interesting to note, however, that lists are used rather differently in Black speech events. Here, listeners do not wait for the completion of a list before making their response. Take this extract from a sermon delivered by Pastor Peterking in a Dudley church where the listing focuses on different forms of transports:

Pastor: Look what God has done for me today. He take me off the donkey.
Congregation: Praise God!
Pastor: He take me off the mule.
Congregation: Praise God!
Pastor: He take me into a car
Congregation: Praise Jesus, glory!

The call-response aspects of this example have, of course, been developed in greater detail in chapter six.

Refrains
We have already considered examples of repetition within refrains in the discussion of 'Wonderful' and 'No woman no Cry' above. The refrain is, of course, a unit of repetition in itself, probably used in all cultural contexts at regular intervals throughout a song. In many Black contexts, however, the refrain is an integral part of storytelling and will be used either to introduce a particular character or a particular theme. Consentino (1982: 138-141) illustrates the centrality of such refrains in a West African Krio story called 'A Witch Evades Justice' which centres on a couple whose children keep on dying and the relatives' desire to find the

family member responsible for this by means of divination. The father is the main suspect and both the narrator, Mama Audu, and the audience assume his role in the following refrain:

Audience:	If it's me-o.
Audience:	Kpana, if it's me, if it's me-o. If it's really me, if it's me-o. Oh my father. If it's really me, if it's me (You don't let it drop, okay; you people: 'If it's me ... ')
Audience:	If it's me. If it's me-o.
	If it's me. If it's me-o.
Audience:	If it's really me, then it's me, but if it really isn't me, then it isn't me. If it's me. If it's me-o.
Audience:	If it's me. If it's me-o.
Audience:	Kpana, if it's me, if it's me-o. If it's really me, if it's me-o. Oh my father. If it's really me, if it's
Audience:	If it's me. If it's me-o. If it's me. If it's me-o.

This refrain is used to mark the appearance of the children's father throughout the storytelling performance.

Storytelling in the Bahamas provides another context for refrains. Crowley (1966: 22-24) describes how the short song or 'sing' may simply be a phrase or two in length, but is usually repeated several times during the telling of the motif. For example "I sharpen m'razor, shee-shaw..." which can be used in any story where the devil or another villain is preparing to engage in acts of violence. In complex songs, it may be sung by successive characters, indicating the progress of the story or actually furthering the narration.

Proverbs and Riddles

Also highly fixed in form are proverbs and riddles, formulaic uses of language which convey meanings without direct explication. In Black communities in the diaspora, they form an important part of an inherited oral tradition. They have been discussed in an African context, for instance, by Finnegan (1970) and Okpewho (1992); in a Caribbean context by Abrahams (1972c), Roberts (1988) and

Watson (1991); in an American context by Mitchell (1986); and in Britain by Jackson (1986).

Proverbs, also referred to as sayings, are widely used in conversation in African cultures. The Nigerian novelist, Chinua Achebe, illustrates this point from an extract in his book *Things fall Apart* (1958: 5-6):

> Having spoken plainly so far, Okoye said the next half dozen sentences in proverbs. Among the Igbo the art of conversation is regarded very highly, and proverbs are the palm-oil with which words are eaten.

In Africa, certain proverbs come from folk tales. For example, the Nigerian proverb, "The person carrying a burden should know what the burden is," originated from a folk tale about a thief who stole some goods and expected someone to help him carry the goods. The most common proverbs relate to the natural environment, the world of animals and observations about human conduct, for example, the Hausa proverb which deals with human peculiarities, "The want of work to do makes a man get up early to salute his enemy" (One will do anything when desperate).

Watson (1991) describes Jamaican proverbs as being sometimes allegorical and poetic. They are frequently based on characters which symbolise Black people and their struggles and include goats (nanny-goats or ram-goats), spiders (or Anansi) and the turkey or vulture (Jankrow) who outwit their foes. For example, "What sweet nanny-goat will run him belly" (even though the things the nanny goat eats taste good she may have a stomach upset) is an appeal for caution: many situations that at first sight seem appealing may turn out to have dire consequences.

Riddles are similar to proverbs in that both are witty and poetic in composition and are also repeated over time and space. However, there are some differences between the two structures. As Edwards & Sienkewicz (1990: 172) explain:

155

The referent of a proverb is clear from the context; the riddle must supply its own referent. Furthermore, while both riddles and proverbs have two or more elements in their description, these metaphoric elements behave quite differently in the two genres. The familiarity of the elements contained within a proverb is such that the listener immediately recognises a pattern. The intent of the riddle, in contrast, is confusion, at least until the answer is provided.

Riddling sessions can consist of small or large groups, They usually take place when the evening meal is over and the immediate or extended family is gathered to relax. They are often introduced with an opening formula, such as the following example from Jamaica:

Riddle me dis riddle me dat, guess me this riddle and p'raps not.

This introduction sets the stage for the analogy which follows. The riddler then issues a challenge to the audience to supply the appropriate solution. For example, the Benin riddle "my father eats with his anus and defecates through his mouth," for which the answer is gun (Herskovits & Herskovits1958: 13).

The successful riddle surprises one and all by making a comparison between people or objects that are not normally associated with one another. For example, the Jamaican riddle "Send boy to fetch doctor, doctor come before boy" is explained as a boy who is sent up a tree to get a coconut who throws down the coconut before descending himself. "Going up to town all cry. Coming home they are silent" describes the sound of feet in the damp of the early morning as compared with the hot dry afternoon (Beckwith 1929: 220 ff).

Functions of Repetition
The functions of repetition are many and varied and have already been hinted at in the discussion of the different forms which it can take. In this part of the chapter, however, we look in particular at

the ways in which repetition provides scaffolding in Black speech events for both performer and audience, by emphasising shared values and by contributing to the dramatic effect or adding humour to the performance.

Composition in Performance

As we have already indicated, repetition allows performers to think what they are going to say next, a process first described by Parry (1930) as 'composition in performance'. The various different forms of repetition examined above, from formulae to lists, from thematic repetition to near repetition, provide both the structure and the building blocks for performance. With these as foundations, performers are able to improvise, to combine the different elements in new and interesting ways. In discussing the functions of repetition, Tannen (1989: 48) says:

> Repetition enables a speaker to produce language in a more efficient, less energy-draining way. It facilitates the production of more language, more fluency. For individuals and cultures that value verbosity and wish to avoid silences in casual conversation ... repetition is a resource for producing ample talk, both by providing material for talk and by enabling talk through automaticity.

The notion of the formula is often invoked in discussion of composition in performance. Parry (1930: 80), writing of the Homeric epic tradition, describes a formula as 'a group of words which is regularly employed under the same metrical conditions to express a given essential idea'. The use of formulae, however, is by no means limited to Greek epic poetry: it is a regular feature of many different kinds of oral performance.

Formulae are often thought of as the building blocks for a performance. By being able to resort to many well known words, phrases and sentences, the performer has time to think ahead. Formulae are used in a wide variety of contexts in Black discourse. Take the following prayer of a school teacher reported by Heath (1988: 102) in Tracton, America:

157

We thank thee for watchin' over us, kind heavenly father
Through the night
We thank thee, oh Lord for leading' 'n guidin' us
We thank thee kind heavenly father for your strong arm protection
around us ...
Oh Lord, I ask thee, Oh Lord to take care of my children, Lord,
wherever they may be ...

The formulaic vocatives, *Oh Lord* and *kind heavenly father*
appear repeatedly throughout the prayer, giving the performer the
necessary time to consider what to say next (see also Finnegan
1970: 457 for a discussion of the use of formulae in African
prayer).

Formulae are particularly important to musical or metrical
performances. In the African-American tradition, epic poems or
toasts, for instance, are usually delivered in rhyming couplets,
with four stresses to the line. The competent toaster can choose
between a number of formulae to end a line which will ensure a
good rhyme. Thus a gun becomes a 45, a 44 or a 38 depending on
which rhyme is needed.

Erickson (1984: 93-94) explains the strategies employed in Black
speech by referring to the classical Greek oral tradition, described
by Aristotle. The term prosographia was used by Aristotle for
commonplace topics or themes which have clusters of related
details. Erickson believes that the purpose of the speaker is to
persuade and arouse the emotions of the audience by means of
commonplace themes. The reliance on the familiar allows the
performer to think ahead. The audience, for their part, is given a
framework for the appreciation of the performance in which
familiarity is an important prop for memorability. In many
African oral narratives, for example, certain phrases, lines and
even the whole framework of details are used repeatedly for
constructing successive stages in the story (Okpewho 1992: 74).
Crowley (1966), shows how in Bahamian storytelling members of
the audience will sometimes complete the narrator's song or even
take on the role of characters in the story. This level of familiarity
with the subject matter allows a high level of participation.

The contexts of most speech events are fixed and associated with specific structures which provide a baseline for composition. The sermon is an obvious example. As previously mentioned in chapter four, the rigid order of the service is in marked contrast with the degree of extemporization which takes place. Thus Holt (1972: 191) states, that the Black Church "has a ritual nearly as rigid and unvarying as that used by the Catholic and High Lutheran services". Davies (1985: 77) makes essentially the same point in describing the 'performed African-American sermon' as a series of repeated phrases. It is interesting, however, to note that, while the overall structure for the service is invariable, this very stability serves as a prop for composition in performance.

Reinforcing Group Values

Repetition also functions on an interactional level. Repeating the words, phrases or sentences of others shows responsiveness and support. Shared meanings and shared assumptions help to forge the bonds between performer and audience, uniting them in a single purpose, as part of one organic whole. Repetition can be used as an important aid to learning. It clearly helps the audience to memorise the speaker's message. It can also be used to impart the collective wisdom of the group, especially in the case of larger units such as proverbs and riddles.

Proverbs are repeatable, and contain a shared meaning which is immediately understood by members of the community. They rely on certain cultural themes, for example, parental authority over children. Those who show disrespect or otherwise carelessly challenge parents by 'back-chat' (talking back) could invoke a proverbial response such as 'two bull cyaan reign in a one pen' (two people cannot have authority under one roof). Proverbs are also often used to cross the generational gap and to unite old and young. 'See and blind, hear and deaf', for instance, is a proverb commonly invoked by older Caribbean and Black British to advocate discretion: whatever you see or hear, it is best to mind your own business.

There are important differences in the social motivation for proverbs and riddles. The aim of proverbs is to support group solidarity by reinforcing the shared values of the group. Riddles, on the other hand, explore ambiguous and disturbing aspects of life which potentially threaten community ideals. Riddles tend to deal with conceptual borderlines, such as exploration of sexual taboo or death. Abrahams (1972c), for instance, discusses riddling sessions at wakes in St Vincent. He suggests that riddling and other kinds of play capitalise on embarrassment and that death is the ultimate embarrassment:

> Because it leads to the most profound disorientation and socio-psychological confusion. Riddles, games, and stories, by re-enacting embarrassment-producing rudeness, help to anatomise the entire confusion or social disruption problem and to replay it in forms in which the participants can feel that the disorienting forces are under control (1972c: 191).

Riddles are also an important form of entertainment and offer participants the opportunity to spend time together in an enjoyable way. They help to bond people together as a group who share the same cultural values. They are highly participatory as no one person dominates. The person attempting to provide the solution is an active partner.

The Crescendo Effect

Repetition has its own aesthetic. Its usefulness lies not simply in helping the orator, the preacher or the toaster to think on their feet, nor in imprinting a message in the minds of the audience. It is a powerful stylistic device for the oral artist who wishes to create dramatic effect. Each repetition is accompanied by a crescendo, leading to a climax which allows the speaker to hold the floor, to sway the audience, to stir up emotion or score a point.

Prosodic features or the tonal semantics already described in chapter six, including pitch, stress and tone, also play a critical role in creating the dramatic effect associated with repetition. The dramatic effects of prosody are a crucial part of repetition in a variety of speech events. However, they are particularly evident in

Black preaching. Take, for instance, the call of Pastor Peterking of the Dudley Church (repeated eleven times in all) and the responses of the congregation which grow progressively louder until they reach a dramatic climax:

Pastor: Let the Church say thank you Jesus (quiet)
Congregation: Thank you Jesus (quiet)
Pastor: Let theChurch say thank you Jesus (slightly louder)
Congregation: Thank you Jesus (slightly louder)
Pastor: Let the Church say thank you Jesus (slightly louder)
Congregation: Thank you Jesus (slightly louder)
Pastor: Let the Church say thank you Jesus (loud)
Congregation: Thank you Jesus (loud)
Pastor: Let the Church say thank you Jesus (loud)
Congregation: Thank you Jesus (loud)
Pastor: Let the Church say thank you Jesus (even louder)
Congregation: Thank you Jesus (even louder)
Pastor: Let the Church say thank you Jesus (even louder)
Congregation: Thank you Jesus (even louder)
Pastor: Let the Church say thank you Jesus (even louder)
Congregation: Thank you Jesus (even louder)
Pastor: Let the Church say thank you Jesus (very loud)
Congregation: Thank you Jesus (very loud)
Pastor: Let the Church say thank you Jesus (very loud)
Congregation: Thank you Jesus (very loud)
Pastor: Let the Church say thank you Jesus (very loud indeed)
Congregation: Thank you Jesus (very loud indeed)

Both the preacher and the congregation are involved in repetitious dialogue. Intonation, stress, tone of voice and other paralinguistic signals all contribute to a powerful and unmistakable crescendo. As Rosenberg (1988: 151) points out in relation to African-American sermons, 'Repetition not only comforts...but it adds to the mounting emotional intensity'.

The level of repetitive hand-clapping in some Black Pentecostal churches can significantly add to this emotional intensity. The different styles of hand-clapping which vary according to the rhythm of the song would appear to be an African retention. As

161

Oozthuizen (1979: 21) observes in a discussion of hand-clapping in Africa:

In some traditional societies, ancestors were approached by hand-clapping. Hand-clapping usually takes place not only when they dance, but when they remain standing in one place.

Prosodic features which contribute to the dramatic climax are also apparent in the speeches of Black politicians. Take the following example from Jesse Jackson in the 1988 Democratic National Convention, in which he repeats and elaborates the idea of a better world by listing the different professions:

> Dream of teachers who teach for life and not for living
> Dream of doctors who are more concerned about public health than private wealth
> Dream of lawyers more concerned about justice than a judgeship
> Dream of preachers who are concerned more about prophecy than profiteering.

Here we see a repetitive structure which starts with the imperative *dream*, continues with a profession and ends with a subordinate clause which, in all but one case, stresses 'concern'. The repetition is marked throughout by heightened pitch on the first part of the sentence and extra stress on contrasting features. Note also how alliteration, assonance and rhyme heighten the dramatic impact of the repetition still further. Equally important, there is a gradual crescendo from start to finish of this segment of the speech which creates feelings of anticipation in the audience and holds them in rapped attention.

The crescendo effect is not solely confined to formal performances but is also an important aspect of informal speech. Hansell and Ajirotutu (1982: 92, cited in Tannen 1989: 80), for instance, discuss an African-American teenager who adopts a 'public address' style similar to that used by Black preachers and politicians. Often speakers in this context use not only exact repetition but also parallelism to develop their point. Thus in the following example, the speaker uses a parallel built on the construction "X is a dog".

Now they make it look like Wallace is a dog
and Nixon is the next dog
and Humphrey is well...[laughter] you know
a little bit higher than the other two dogs [laughter] but he's still a dog

Prosodic features of pitch, stress and rhythm draw attention to the parallel and help create a dramatic effect.

Erikson (1984: 140 ff) also examines the way in which repetition is used to create a dramatic climax in the banter of African-American youth.

Joe:	He was talking about how they was corruptin' the votin' **they threw him <u>out</u>**
Al: Yeah	(moderate volume)
Denise:	He told us about the B.Y.F. meeting too
Joe:	**<u>Thew</u> him out** (louder)
Al:	Uh hum (Not much louder than first intervention)
Jim:	You know, what this dude
Joe:	I mean (still louder)
	threw him out. I don't just mean just put him, I mean (still louder)
	THEW HIM OUT! (loudest)
Group:	(loud general laughter)

Erickson comments on the way in which Joe shifts the contrastive stress from the final position in the first utterance of '*they threw him <u>out</u>* ' to the initial position in *<u>Thew</u> him out*' in the first and second repetition. He also comments on the shift from the more formal *threw* to the colloquial *thew*. Each instance is louder than the one before, achieving a heightened response, culminating in the outburst of loud general laughter, the final validation from the audience.

A similar example can be cited from the Dudley data as Terry and Elvis discuss various instances of conflict with their families and the punitive measures taken by their parents.

Terry: **I've never been locked out**
Elvis: We were just talking about that
Terry: **I've never been locked out** (louder)
Elvis: My ole man, my ole man, he lock me out once, right. I went to watch a video and I came back at four ...
Terry: **I've never been locked out by my parents** (louder).

Here each repetition of *'I've never been locked out'* is louder than the last. This use of crescendo enables Terry to hold the floor and ensure that his point is made.

Repetition can also add to the drama of performance by injecting an element of humour. As Reisman (1974: 121) points out:

> To have something to say that is worth hearing and also repeatable implies that it is fairly short, and as a result, there is a process of condensation and allusion at work all the time. One is expected to catch the meaning. And conversely there is a feeling that undue explicitness implies a dull person.

The following extract from Pastor Peterking in Dudley illustrates this humorous use of repetition. The pastor is making a play on the contrast between physical and spiritual beauty:

Pastor: I have two sisters. One said she wanted to marry a *pretty* man and she did marry a *pretty* man [pause] him *ugly* ...
Congregation: (roars with laughter)
Pastor: My other sister, she marry a man who wasn't an oil painting, if you know what I mean
Congregation: (laughter)
Pastor: But the man's way was so *pretty*.

Pastor Peterking has chosen a word which Reisman (1974 121): would describe as 'free flowing' and which allows the audience to interpret the meaning in their own way. The use of *pretty* to describe a man is, in itself, amusing. Each repetition of *pretty* heightens the humour. The juxtaposition of *pretty* and *ugly* adds further to this effect. Note, too, the fact, that Pastor Peter- king's delivery of the punch line in each comment was marked by distinctive creole intonation and, in the first instance, also by creole syntax. This has the effect of bonding the pastor and the congregation, and further underlying shared experiences and expectations.

Assonance and alliteration also form the focus of word-play within humorous repetition. Erickson (1984 141), for instance, shows, in a discussion of a vote about the extermination of rats in the neighbourhood, how Ed makes a pun on the words *no* and *know:*

Ed: .... They voted
        no ... now why I don't
        know... they just voted
        no.

As Erickson indicates, each repetition was rhythmically accentuated; the pitch and stress of each /no/ was the same at each repetition

In all these cases - in sermons, songs, political speeches or the cut and thrust of peer group conversation - repetition is used to build up atmosphere, to hold the stage, to sway the emotions.

Conclusion
In looking at the range of forms which repetition takes, it is possible to make two main observations. First, repetition is expressed in many different ways: from simple repetition to 'elaborate variation'; and in units which range in length from a single word to a whole refrain. Second, these different forms of repetition are combined in many different ways. It is not the case, for instance, that certain forms of repetition are associated with certain speech events. The tendency of western, literate observers to dismiss repetition as unsophisticated and tedious is extremely short-sighted.

Closer examination of a range of oral performances points clearly to the ways in which many different kinds of repetition are skilfully interwoven to fulfil a number of functions and to achieve a range of stylistic effects. Repetition - from the reduplication of words to the shared appreciation of much longer units - permeates oral language. It allows performers to think on their feet. It provides the framework and stability for enormous creativity. It helps the audience to become part of the performance. It helps to reinforce shared group values. It also creates humour. And last, but by no means, least, it is responsible for creating dramatic effect. By combining repetition with crescendo, the oral artist can hold attention, inspire and excite, amuse and entertain.

CHAPTER 8

CONCLUSION

ಬ ಬ ಬ

In the course of this book I have attempted to examine a range of language behaviours of Black people in the diaspora. The underlying assumption has been that elements of African ways of speaking are still very much a part of the cultural heritage of Black people in the Caribbean, America and Britain and that a greater understanding of these ways of speaking has the potential to improve both the status of Black speech and inter-cultural communication.

An important starting point in chapter two was to trace the history of Black language in the diaspora. African slaves came in the main from West Africa where thousands of different languages were spoken and diverse cultural practices existed. While some writers have viewed these differences as obstacles to social cohesion others have pointed to the strong underlying similarities in ways of thinking, behaving and speaking (cf Levine 1977).

Africans in the New World were subjected to very similar experiences. Both societies were exposed to European colonization; slavery had a profound impact on political, social and economic life; Blacks struggled for equality and resisted White oppression over the centuries. This culture of resistance is characterised by many African retentions in religion, language and behaviour.

This is not to suggest, however, that history followed precisely the same route in the Caribbean and America. In the Caribbean, Africans formed the majority, a factor which no doubt explains why, while the legacy of colonialism is still evident, almost all Caribbean countries are now controlled by politicians of African descent. In America, Blacks form a minority population and have always had limited access to political power. It is interesting to note that, although African- Americans have more wealth and influence than at any other time since their enslavement, as a group they still remain at the bottom of the social and economic ladder.

Most British Blacks have come to Britain via the Caribbean. The fact that they form a minority population in Britain means that their experience is possibly closer to that of African-Americans than African Caribbeans. There is certainly no shortage of evidence of the widespread racism to which they have been exposed in the areas of housing, employment and education (cf Brown 1985.

The nature and origins of the linguistic heritage of Africans in the diaspora were explored in chapter three. The linguistic history of the Caribbean is complex. The contact between many different peoples, speaking many different languages, gave rise first to a pidgin, a greatly reduced form of communication. Over time, children who grew up speaking the pidgin as their first language, expanded the simplified grammar into a creole capable of expressing all their communication needs. For the purposes of this Book, discussion has focused primarily on Jamaica, the island from which the majority of British Blacks first came. Here the vocabulary base is predominantly English, though many African elements of phonology and syntax have been retained. The relative importance of African influence is a question that has been hotly debated over the years (cf Alleyne 1980). Another area of contention is the current status of Jamaican and other Caribbean creoles. Changes brought about by education and social and economic development have given rise to such a wide range of linguistic variation that writers such as De Camp (1971b) have suggested that the present situation should be described in terms of a post-creole continuum; while others propose that the variation is better explained in terms of code-switching between a broad creole and the standard.

The historical development of Black English Vernacular (or BEV) of African-Americans is similar to that of Caribbean creoles. In America, however, probably because Whites outnumbered Blacks, a widespread creole either failed to develop or went through a rapid process of decreolization. There is currently widespread disagreement as to whether Black English is diverging from or converging towards standard English. Developments such as desegregation would suggest that BEV might be moving closer to the standard; the continuing racism which African-Americans experience, however, might well result in an accentuation of linguistic difference as a symbol of resistance.

Patterns of language use in Britain differ in important respects from those in both America and the Caribbean. The proportion of Black speakers in Britain is considerably smaller than in either of the two other destinations for Africans in the diaspora. While initially it was assumed that British Blacks had become linguistically assimilated, further research has shown that they are able to speak in varying degrees a distinct variety known as Patois. Their level of competence, and frequency and patterns of usage are determined by a number of factors, the most important of which is social network. Those speakers whose social life is firmly rooted in the Black community use Patois more frequently and in a wider range of situations; they are also the most competent Patois speakers.

An understanding of attitudes towards Black language is essential to any discussion of inter-cultural communication. Caribbean creoles have a legacy of low status. They are often referred to as 'bad' or 'broken' and viewed as the language of the poor, uneducated masses. The same kind of negative attitudes can be found in relation to BEV. In the 1960s, for instance, there was particularly acrimonious debate between deficit and difference theorists. The deficit hypothesis postulated that linguistic differences between Black and White children were a symptom of linguistic and cognitive deprivation which could only be remedied by teaching Black children to speak standard English. The difference hypothesis, in contrast, postulated that Black English was a perfectly rule-governed linguistic system which fulfilled all the communication needs of its speakers: it was different from the standard but in no way linguistically deficient.

Given the widespread prejudice against any variety which departs from the standard (cf Edwards 1989), it is not surprising to find that the same prejudices documented for the Caribbean and America have also been widespread in Britain (cf Edwards and Tomlin 1986). While some attempts have been made to promote more favourable attitudes towards Patois in school, various commentators (eg Carby 1980; Stone 1981) have pointed to the cosmetic nature of such initiatives and the fact that these do not address the wider social and political issues.

It is important to remember, however, that while Black people in all three locations have internalised these negative attitudes towards their speech, they also express a high level of ambivalence. Overt acceptance of the prestige associated with the language of the White oppressors is only part of the story. Black ways of speaking are a symbol of the resistance of many Black speakers to linguistic and cultural assimilation. As such, they are associated with qualities such as sincerity and trustworthiness.

In chapters four and five, we moved from the history and description of Black language to an ethnography of speaking. Like other oral cultures, Africans in the diaspora have enormous respect for 'men of words' (cf Abrahams 1970). Black speech events can be divided into two main categories: bad talk and sweet talk. Bad talk which includes such speech events as ritual invective and boasting, refers to performances where humour and repartee are used to challenge accepted community mores. Sweet talk, in contrast, is carried out in more respectable settings and does not pose a threat to the status quo. It includes such speech events as sermons, testimonies, political speeches and dub poetry. Both types of speech events, however, reinforce the social values of the group, one by verbalising them, the other by acting as a valve for anti-social impulse. Sometimes there is no clear boundary between sweet talk and bad talk. Throwing words is a case in point. It involves the use of indirect comments to slander or rebuke. However, it can be used to equal effect among youths on street corners and from the preacher in the pulpit.

Speech events serve a number of different functions. They reinforce the cultural values of Black people. They enable young performers to establish a place for themselves in the pecking order, and to develop the skills which they need for survival in their community. They also entertain.

The communal and interactive aspect of Black speech events was explored further in the discussion of call and response in chapter six. Call-response is evident in both speech and music. It requires the audience to echo or add to the words of the performer and can take a variety of forms, including co-signing, on t, encouraging, repetition and completer statements. It can also take the form of co-narration where speakers complete each other's statement or individual call-response, where performers respond to their own calls.

As well as the more structured call-response devices, there is considerable overlap between speakers which can be found in both sacred and secular contexts. Often the performer uses shared knowledge or special intonation to cue the audience. Sometimes intonation or 'tonal semantics' is used as a cue for audience response. The communal nature of performances illustrate the highly interactive style of Black speech events.

The use of call-response also reflects the symbiotic relationship between the audience and performer. Such a relationship depends to a great extent on shared experiences and group solidarity.

Repetition is another recurrent feature of Black speech events, explored in chapter seven. It takes a number of different forms, from the simple repetition of single words or phrases to proverbs and riddles. These different forms of repetition are combined in several different ways.

Detailed analysis reveals that repetititon fulfils a number of functions. It allows performers to improvise and provides a platform for creativity. It enables the audience to become a part of the performance. It helps to forge the bonds of shared group values. It creates dramatic effect: by combining repetition with crescendo, the oral artists captivate the attention of the audience.

The examples and analysis offered as part of the present discussion have had two main aims. The first has been to underline the common features of Black language behaviour in three different locations - the Caribbean, America and Britain - separated both in time and space from their African antecedents. These behaviours have much in common with oral cultures in other parts of the world. There is, however, a great deal of variation within oral cultures (cf Edwards & Sienkewicz 1990): Athabaskans behave very differently from African-Americans, for instance, even though both groups live in North America. The preceding pages have attempted to trace the common ancestry and parallel development of Black ways of speaking in the diaspora.

The second aim has been to document more fully the forms and functions of Black language in Britain. While African-Caribbean and African-American speech events have received considerable attention in the literature, the main focus within Britain has been to describe linguistic variation rather than to attempt an ethnography of speaking. Drawing on my insider status, I have been able to document in both secular and sacred contexts a wide range of speech events which have received little or no attention in the past. I have also attempted to extend a discussion which is normally reserved for speech to music, demonstrating that the same stylistic principles and cultural norms operate in both contexts.

Cross-Cultural Communication
Another recurrent feature of the preceding chapters is the potential for misunderstanding which exists when co-existent groups differ in their expectations as to how words should be used. This is an area which clearly has enormous implications for the success or otherwise of intergroup relations.

Cultural identity can be defined as an individual's strong, voluntary attachment to a group and to its values as a result of some real link with the past. When two cultures come into contact, there is often a mismatch resulting in misunderstanding and feelings of unease (McDonald 1989). This mismatch does not pose a serious problem for cultures whose boundaries are well-defined. However, when cultural identities are less clear or, when a minority has been forced into biculturalism through conquest or economic and political pressure, the differences between the two cultures can become a source of misunderstanding and continued oppression for the less powerful. This is certainly the case with Black minority communities in America and Britain.

Expectations about appropriate behaviour in conversation are determined to a great extent by our cultural experiences which are mainly unconscious. Misunderstanding takes place when one group interacts with another whose cultural experience is different. For example, certain native American groups wait several minutes before responding or taking a turn in conversation (Saville-Troike 1982: 23) whilst, in African-Caribbean conversation, it is acceptable for several people to speak at the same time (Reisman 1974: 113-114). Similarly, visual cues can also vary cross-culturally, causing misunderstanding. For instance, in some cultures it is customary to show attention by looking away, while, in others, people who avert their gaze are thought to be uninterested (cf Corson 1993: 57).

The Oral-Literate Continuum
At the beginning of this thesis we examined the oral-literate continuum in relation to Black culture. As we have already indicated Black culture is essentially an oral one However, it has been influenced by literacy and is on a continuum between orality and literacy In this chapter, we argue that the same continuum plays an important role in cross-cultural communication.

One of the main features of literate discourse is that the writer needs to be explicit, because the reader cannot seek clarification. Communication does not need to be face to face; it can take place across time and space. For this reason, writing tends to be more condensed than speech. Relationships between different parts of written discourse are made explicit and the effect is thus of thoughts being developed in a linear way.

Oral discourse, in contrast, is marked by interaction with listeners, who are free to question the speaker on any points which need to be explained. There is evidence that the oral discourse of literate speakers is heavily influenced by written language (Perera 1984). In societies where the influence of the written word is less pronounced, however, it is possible to discern discourse patterns which are often markedly different.

Different Discourse Style
Difference between discourse styles influenced by oral and literate traditions have considerable potential for causing cross-cultural misunderstanding. This misunderstanding takes place in three main areas: the highly participative nature of interation in oral cultures; the different organising principles; and the different stylistic preferences. Let us consider first the different levels of participation at the two ends of the oral-literate continuum. Tannen (1980: 3) makes a useful distinction between two main styles in conversation which she calls 'high involvement' and 'high considerateness'. She observes that these two styles correspond to the oral-literate continuum. High involvement speakers use the interactive strategies reminiscent of oral cultures. High considerateness speakers, in contrast, place emphasis on content and individual expression and use strategies reminiscent of literate culture. This difference is particularly apparent in cross-cultural discourse. High considerateness participants allow speakers to make their point without interruption. High involvement speakers, in contrast, behave quite differently.

This distinction can be usefully applied to Black speakers who use a high involvement style and mainstream Whites who favour high considerateness. Black oral culture, as we have seen, is characterised by the process of call-response which involves a high level of interaction between speaker and listener in which all the speaker's statements are punctuated by comments from the listener. In inter-racial settings in America and Britain, however, the call-response behaviours of Black speakers sometimes give rise to serious misunderstandings between Whites and Blacks. Kochman (1981), for instance, suggests that, when a Black speaker holds the floor, the polite attention offered by White interlocutors is likely to be interpreted as inattention by Black speakers. To rectify the situation, Black speakers may intersperse their contributions with comments such as 'Do you know what I'm saying'? or 'Do you know what I mean'? White interlocutors, however, may find such interventions annoying and may resent the implication that they do not understand or are not listening when in fact this is not the case. They are often unaware that the Black speaker is merely requesting them to respond. Conversely, problems arise when the White speaker is holding the floor. Responses from Black listeners to 'Go ahead' or 'tell it as it is' may be received as an unwelcome distraction.

Erickson (1984: 98) describes an example of this kind of misunderstanding in a meeting between African-American community representatives and White faculty members. The African-American presented their arguments using a highly interactive style of discourse which drew on other Black members of the audience. Many White faculty members, however, found this style difficult to cope with. As one White member said, 'I didn't come here to listen to a Baptist's prayer meeting.' A middle class Black faculty member responded with 'You just insulted my religion' producing laughter and applause on the part of the community. This reaction confirmed the White participants' impression that 'those people were unreasonable' and that the oral discourse style of the community representatives was incoherent and incomprehensible. The Black representatives, in turn, considered the White faculty members to be unreasonable.

Kochman (1981) makes similar observations about Black discourse styles. The general rule for turn-taking in Black discourse, is 'interrupt when you can' and this is not perceived as an infringement of others' rights. Consequently, there is a high level of simultaneous and overlapping speech (cf Reisman 1974) involving repetition both for rhetorical emphasis and as a way of being heard.

As Kochman (1981: 18) points out:

The modes of behaviour that Blacks and Whites consider appropriate for engaging in public debate on an issue differ in their stance and level of spiritual intensity. The black mode - that of Black community people - is high-keyed; animated, interpersonal and confrontational. The white mode - that of the middle class - is relatively low-keyed; dispassionate, impersonal, and non-challenging. The first is characteristic of involvement; it is heated loud, and generates affect. The second is characteristic of detachment and is cool, quiet, and without affect.

In a study of Black and White debating styles in inter-racial classrooms in America, Kochman (1981: 34-35) found that the African-American students reflect the normal patterns of interaction in their community where:

Those with greater ability tend to dominate the proceedings as well as offer themselves as contenders against whom others can test their skills ... Blacks do not simply debate an idea; they debate the person debating the idea.

In contrast, Whites 'tend to debate the idea rather than the person debating the idea'. This enables those who disagreee to enter into the discussion without having to match the forcefulness of the opposition, since they are not in direct confrontation. This mode allows a lot more involvement, since participation is not dependent upon those who possess strong debating skills.

In such instances, a Black student with strong debating skills may be labelled as aggressive by a teacher using White literate standards. Alternatively, a White student who does not feel comfortable with this style of debating may decide to opt out of the discussion when a Black student makes a more personal challenge.

Ways with words are inevitably related to broader social patterns. Boykin (1978), suggests that Black home environment provides

176

an abundance of stimulation, intensity and variation. There tends to be a relatively higher noise level with television and stereophonic music playing. Often, large numbers of people occupy a living space, with a variety of activities taking place. Outside the home, in Black communities in Africa, the Caribbean, America and Britain, social occasions such as weddings and church services are also characteristically vibrant.

A White [Jewish] member of a Black Pentecostal church describes the effects of Black worship patterns on White visitors thus:

> The pumping of the repetitious phrase 'Praise God', the limitless singing of an 'old-time chorus' and the non-stop clapping of hands could prove to be uncomfortable for a White person.

In addition, he points out that the high volume of music and singing and the physical movement of individual church members during some 'electrifying services' can be an unusual experience for the White observer. He also comments on the call-response elements and dynamic delivery of Black preaching style:

> By the time the preacher is ready to begin his sermon a sense of relief stirs within the White person, but the security is shattered by the forceful preaching and the loud frequent 'Amens' and 'Yeses' from the congregation. The whole presentation has a dazzling effect on the unsuspecting White individual. At times sermons are not fully appreciated because of foreign anecdotes, and to have the message interpreted by a helpful neighbour is not as rewarding or effective (Brooks 1985: 77).

A second area in which different styles have potential for cross-cultural misunderstanding relates to the organisation of discourse. White observers often characterize Black speech as episodic, disconnected and lacking in organizing principles. As Smitherman (1977: 148) explains:

The relating of events (real or hypothetical) becomes a Black rhetorical strategy to explain a point, to persuade holders of opposing views to one's own point of view, and in general to 'win friends and influence people'. This meandering away from the 'point' takes the listener on episodic journeys...it all eventually leads back to the source. Though highly applauded by Blacks, this narrative linguistic style is exasperating to Whites who wish you'd be direct and hurry up and get to the point.

Michaels and Collins (1984), make a similar point when they examine the key classroom activity of 'sharing time' where children give a narrative account of some past event. They identify differences in discourse style between White and Black children. White children tend to use a topic-centred style in which a single clearly identified topic is chosen and temporal and spatial developments are clearly indicated. In contrast to the topic-centred style, the Black children, and particularly the Black girls, tend to use a 'topic associating' or an 'episodic style', consisting of a series of implicitly associated topics. Links between topics tend to be marked by intonation but White listeners are often insensitive to these markers.

Erickson (1984) also draws attention to this phenomenon in a study of coherence strategies in African-American adolescents. He shows that the relationship between topics or main points is rarely explicitly stated: rather, implicit themes are inferred from a series of concrete anecdotes.

A third area of potential misunderstanding concerns the use of stylistic devices which many White observers dismiss as 'flowery', 'excessive' or even 'obsequious'. Black language makes widespread use of metaphor and hyperbole. It is also the product of a culture in which praise and blame are well-developed verbal traditions (cf Edwards & Sienkewicz 1990). Praise can focus on the self, as in the boasting behaviour of the calypso, or on others, as in the speech making which marks important social events such as weddings. As we saw in chapter four, blame can take the form of indirect censure in 'throwing words' or the more public acts of tantalizing and busing. Many White observers find speech events which focus on blame uncouth and embarrassing. Speech events which focus on praise are dismissed as obsequious and make them feel uncomfortable. In both cases, there is a tendency to interpret Black speech events through a White cultural matrix and a failure to perceive their vital role in maintaining social equilibrium by articulating the values of the group.

Education

Cross-cultural misunderstanding has particularly serious implications in the field of education, one of the most important meeting points for speakers from dominant and minority cultures. To appreciate the ways in which different groups interact, it is important first to explore the broader issue of language in education. The theories of Bourdieu (1966), for instance, are very helpful in showing how the practices of a society are re-invented and perpetuated through language. He introduces the concepts of 'cultural and linguistic capital' to describe the advantages which work in favour of some groups and exclude others. Cultural capital refers to benefits accrued as part of life experiences, peer group contacts and family background, including such things as 'good taste', style, certain kinds of knowledge and presentation of self. Similarly, linguistic capital is more than the competence to produce grammatically well-formed expressions: it includes the ability to produce the right expressions at the right time. The norms for cultural and linguistic capital are determined by the dominant group who possess the economic and social power to reinforce their position in society. The school, of course, is a creation of the dominant culture as it reflects the ideas and values of that culture. The educational system is one which primarily prepares middle-class children from the dominant culture to take part in their own culture.

Middle-class children have access to the standard language and accepted ways with words and are rewarded academically for their cultural and linguistic capital. Users of non-standard varieties are penalised for patterns of language acquired in less prestigious settings.

The negative attitudes towards non-standard speech have a long history but, as we saw in chapter three, gathered momentum in the 1960s and 1970s. The main catalyst for the resurgence in the debate on the validity of non-standard varieties, including Black language, came from Bernstein (1973). He argued that the two language codes, the 'elaborated' and the 'restricted', accounted for the different rates of educational achievement within society. Bernstein's work was widely interpreted as suggesting that the elaborate code could be equated with non-standard speech, a position which has been severely criticised by writers such as Edwards (1979) and Gordon (1981). However, the Bernstein debate is particularly significant for present purposes if analysed within the framework of the oral-literate continuum. His description of the elaborate code as dealing with decontextualized reference has obvious points of similarity with literate discourse while the description of restricted code as context-bound has resonance with the oral tradition. The terms 'elaborated' and 'restricted' are unfortunate not only because they imply a simple division rather than a continuum in which all speakers use both sets of strategies, but because of the underlying assumption that the literate strategies demanded by the educational system are the only route to learning (cf Edwards and Sienkewicz 1990). The fact remains, however, that children with different approaches to learning may receive differential treatment in school.

Often Black minority students approach literacy activities in majority culture classrooms in ways that are inconsistent with school norms but consistent with their own cultural norms and values. The culturally different discourse style of Black students is not recognised in societies such as America and Britain and has enormous consequences for, amongst other things, the development of literacy skills. Heath (1982: 70) points out that:

> In each society, certain kinds of childhood participation in literacy events may precede others. The ways of taking [from print] employed in the school may in turn build directly on the pre-school development, may require substantial adaptation on the part of children, or may even run directly counter to aspects of the community's pattern.

She finds that access to a literate discourse style is not equally easy for all children. Some children are at an advantage as they bring a style that is more compatible with that of the school. In contrast, other children's patterns are inconsistent with those of the school. In a study of the literacy events of children in Trackton, a Black community in America, Heath (1988) shows how individual reading is not highly valued and written text is always discussed and debated among several people. Trackton children develop their language skills by being a party to group discussions rather than in a one-to-one situation of reading a book with an adult.

Aronowitz (1984) also discusses the effect of oral discourse strategies on the acquisition of literacy. He describes the way in which Black children approach school tasks as real-world problems rather than as decontextualized tasks. When answering questions on reading texts, they extend upon the information stated in the paragraph.

The different discourse strategies of Black and White children have already been discussed: White children tend to use a 'topic centred' and Black children a 'topic associating' approach. The fact that White teachers identify more closely with a topic centred approach has serious implications for racial equality.

In the Michaels & Collins (1984) study of 'sharing time' or 'show and tell' in which children are expected to recount something that has happened or talk about something they have brought in from home, the teacher was much more successful in working with children who adopted a topic-centred style. She provided an adult-like model of literate discourse through her questions, clarity and explicitness. However, with the African-American children, she had difficulty in seeing the point and predicting the speaker's direction. She made appropriate interruptions which upset the children's train of thought.

Michaels and Cazden (1986) extend on Michaels and Collins' research on sharing time. They believe that a study of this particular activity provides a mirror into the larger problem of equality in education, since many teachers approach sharing time as an oral preparation for literacy and some children get more practice and informal instruction than others. They found that narratives which use a topic associating or episodic style are perceived more negatively than topic centred narratives.

Differences in non-verbal styles of communication also form an important area of conflict between White teachers and Black students. Non-verbal communication is an essential feature of both oral and literate cultures but varies cross-culturally. Often, the non-verbal styles of Black students are perceived as threatening by teachers who misinterpret their behaviour (cf Dandy 1991). One example frequently quoted as a cause of friction is the way some Black students lower their eyes when confronted by a teacher. This is seen as a sign of respect in Black culture but interpreted as insolence within the context of the mainstream school. Conversely, what Kunjufu (1986: 10) labels the look of defiance, 'the showdown', where a Black student stares intensely at a teacher, may well be a display of hostility. There are other non-verbal cues which can lead to over-reaction by pupils and teachers alike resulting in serious consequences, as indicated in a recent report on exclusions from Nottingham secondary schools (1992: 112):

> Several non-verbal styles of communication often displayed by Black pupils seem to convey specific messages to many teachers that the pupil must be arrogant, insolent, defiant, aggressive, disruptive and 'looking for trouble'. Examples mentioned by teachers in the enquiry schools and documented in research describe the beginning of ongoing conflict: the way they look at you; walking in an exaggerated way; displaying dumb insolence; looking away when challenged; 'sucking and hissing' their teeth...

Dandy (1991) points out that African-American students often interact with each other informally in loud voices and are disciplined for disrupting mainstream classrooms. Similar instances have been reported in Britain. For example, a study of referral and suspension of pupils in Birmingham, claims that Black children often came into conflict with teachers because of

Black children often came into conflict with teachers because of their 'liveliness' (CRE 1985: 10). There can be little doubt that this is an important area of cultural difference.

Future Research

In this Book I have presented Black oral culture as dynamic and vibrant, bearing little resemblance to the view presented in theories of verbal and cultural deprivation in the educational literature of the 1960s and 1970s which still resonates in many schools today. Yet the question of linguistic diversity in the various settings we have considered has usually been approached in terms of the inability of Black students to speak standard English rather than in terms of the rich and varied linguistic culture they bring to school. This view has unfortunate consequences since the emphasis on the values of the dominant culture is likely to lead to negative stereotyping.

Teachers are in a unique position in that they are able to challenge deep-seated values and attitudes. There are many opportunities, for instance, for including Black discourse styles in the classroom. Various studies such as Piestrup (1974), Ladson-Billings (1991) and Foster (1989; 1991) show how Black teachers have successfully used interactive features of Black language such as repetition, alliteration, call and response and rhythm in normal classroom teaching. Foster, in particular, focuses on the way these techniques have engaged not only Black students but White and other minorities in the learning process.

There is, however, a need for further research into how aspects of Black language can be exploited in an educational setting. Developments in this area will help to valorise the oral culture that Black students bring into school. Which features lend themselves best to classroom adaptation? How should they be introduced? What are the reactions of children and parents? Students may well be more likely to appreciate the literate culture of the school if both oral skills and literate strategies are acknowledge and accepted.

The study of Black language has been considered within the framework of the oral-literate continuum, where the oral and literate traditions are interrelated. Whilst orality and literacy merge, the importance attached to the two traditions is different. We have attempted to show that Black culture has retained many aspects of its oral African roots and the spoken word is held in high esteem.

Unfortunately Western literate observers hold orality in very low esteem, as can be seen in the widespread ignorance of Black speech events. Important work has been done in the ethnography of speaking in Africa, America, the Caribbean and Britain. However, much work still remains to be done. A priority within the British context is the documentation of the speech events of British born adolescents in informal peer group settings. To what extent, for instance, do the speech events of British born youth correspond to those of their Caribbean born parents?

Further research on the acquisition of Patois by British Black children is also important. Most research to date has focused on the language of adolescents. But, while we know that the speech of younger children in formal settings such as school approximates loosely to the local White norm, our picture of the language of children who function in predominantly Black settings, such as Pentecostal churches, is much less clear. Other issues which deserve attention include regional variation in Black language in Britain.

As well as the verbal forms of communication, the non-verbal styles of communication form an important area for future research. Black people use many non-verbal cues which are very different from those employed by Whites. We have already indicated that the Black non-verbal styles of communication can lead to conflict between White teachers and Black students. It can also result in misunderstanding in other social contexts such as sacred settings where the physical movement of Black and White Christians differ. It is hoped that future research of Black language style will further reveal its depth, richness and vitality.

REFERENCES

Abrahams, R. D. (1962) Playing the dozens. *Journal of American Folklore* 75: 209-218.

Abrahams, R. D. (1962) The toast: a neglected form of folk narrative. In H.P. Beck (ed.) *Folkore in action: essays for discussion in honour of MacEdward Leach.* Philadelphia: The American Folklore Society, pp 1-11.

Abrahams, R. D. (1967) The shaping of folklore tradition in the British West Indies. *Journal of Inter-American Studies* 1X: 456-80.

Abrahams, R. D. (1970a) The traditions of eloquence in Afro-American communities. *Journal of Inter-American Studies and World Affairs* 12: 505-27.

Abrahams, R. D. (1970b) Patterns of performance in the British West Indies. In N. Szwed & J. Whitten (eds.) *Afro-American Anthropology: Contemporary Perspectives.* New York: The Free Press.

Abrahams, R. D. (1970c) *Deep down in the Jungle: negro narrative folklore from the streets of Philadelphia* (revised edition). Chicago: Aldine.

Abrahams, R. D. (1972a) The training of the man of words in talking sweet. *Language in Society* 1 (1): 15-30.

Abrahams, R. D. (1972b) Joking: the training of the man of words in talking broad. In T Kochman (ed.) *Rappin' and Stylin' Out: Communication in Urban Black America.* Chicago: University of Illinois Press pp.215-40.

Abrahams, R. D. (1972c) The literary study of the riddle. *Texas Studies in Literature and Language* 14: 177-97.

Abrahams, R. D. (1976) *Talking black.* New York: Newbury House.

Abrahams, R. D. (1989) Black talking on the streets. In R. Bauman & J. Sherzer (eds.) *Explorations in the ethnography of speaking*(second edition). Cambridge: Cambridge University Press, pp.240-256.

Achebe, C. (1980) *Things Fall Apart.* New York: Aston-Honor.

Albert, E. M. (1964) 'Rhetoric', 'logic' and 'poetics' in Burundi: Cultural patterning of speech behaviour. *American Anthropologist* 66 (6 (2)): 35-54.

Alleyne, M. (1980) *Comparative Afro-American.* Ann Arbor: Karoma.

Alleyne, M. (1988) *Roots of Jamaican Culture.* London: Pluto.
Arnold, S. (1992) *From scepticism to hope: one black-led church's reponse to social responsibility.* Nottingham: Grove Books Ltd.

Aronowitz, R. (1984) Reading tests as texts. In D. Tannen (ed.) *Coherence in spoken and written discourse.* Norwood, NJ: Ablex, 245-64.

Asamen, J. K. (1989) Afro-American students and academic achievement. In G. L. Berry. & J. K. Asamen (eds.) *Black Students Psychosocial Issues and Academic Achievement.* California: Los Angeles, pp.10-16.

Ash, S. & Myhill, J (1986) Linguistic correlates of inter-ethnic contact. In D. Sankoff (ed.) *Current issues in linguistic theory, diversity and diachrony.* Amsterdam: John Benjamins, pp.33-44.

Association of Teaching of English to Pupils from Overseas (ATEPO) (Birmingham Branch) (1970). *Work Group on West Indian Pupils Report.*

Aswad (1988) Don't turn around *Island Records.* Bailey, B. (1966) *Jamaican creole syntax.* Cambridge: Cambridge University Press.

Bailey, G. & Maynor, N. (1985a) The present tense *to be* in southern black folk speech. *American Speech* 60 195-213.

Bailey, G. & Bassett, M. (1986) Invariant *be* in the lower south. In M. Montgomery & G. Bailey (eds.) *Language variety in the South: Perspectives in black and white.* Tuscaloosa: University of Alabama Press, pp.158-79.

Barrett, L. (1976) *The sun and the drum.* Kingston, Jamaica: Caribbean.

Barrett, L. (1977) *The* Rastafarians. London: Heineman.

Beckwith, M. (1929) *Black roadways.* Chapel Hill, N.C: The University of North Carolina Press.

Bennett Jr, L. (1993) *The shaping of America.* Harmondsworth, Middlesex: Penguin.

Bennett, L. (1966) *Jamaica labrish.* Jamaica: Sangster's Book Stores Ltd.

Bereiter, C. &. Engelmann, S. (1966) *Teaching disadvantaged children in the pre-school.* Englewood Cliffs, New Jersey: Prentice-Hall.

Bernstein, B. (1973) *Class, codes and control.* London: Routledge & Kegan Paul.

Berry, G. L. & Asamen, J .K. (eds.) (1989) *Black students psychosocial issues and academic achievement.* California: Los Angeles: Sage.

Bickerton, D. (1980) Decreolisation and the creole continuum. In A Valderman & A Highfield. (eds.) *Theoretical orientations in creole studies.* New York: Academic Press, pp.109-29.

Bickerton, D. (1984) The language bioprogram hypothesis. *The Behavioural and Brain Sciences* (7): 173-221.

Blair, Rev. (1990) *Marathana.* Sermon delivered at De Montfort Hall, Leicester. Sapphire Video Services Ltd P.O Box 13 Walsall WS3 1TZ

Bloomfield, L. (1933) *Language.* New York: Henry Holt.

Bones, J. (1986) Reggae deejaying and Jamaican Afro-lingua. In D. Sutcliffe & A. Wong (eds)*The language of the Black experience.* Oxford: Basil Blackwell, pp. 52-68.

Bourdieu, P. (1966) L'école conservatrice. *Revue Francaise de Sociologie* 7: 225-26; 330-42; 346-47.

Boykin, W. A. (1978) Psychological behavioural verve in academic task performance: pretheoretical considerations. *Journal of Negro Education* (47): 343-54.

Brooks, I. (1982) *Where do we go from here?* London: Charles Raper.

Brooks, I. (1985) *Another gentleman to the ministry.* Birmingham: West Midlands: Compeer Press.

Brown, C (1985) *Black and white Britain.* London: Policy Studies Institute.

Brown, C. &. Gay., P. (1985) *Racial discrimination: 17 years after the Act.* London: Policy Studies Institute.

Brown, C. (1965) *Manchild in the promised land.* New York: Signet.

Brown, H. R. (1969) *Die nigger die!* New York: The Dial Press.

Callendar, C. & Humphrey, C. (1991)*The art of insult.* Interview with Atilla the Stockbroker. Radio 4 SLN11791FQOO73.

Callender, C. & Cameron. D. (1990) Responsive listening as a part of religious rhetoric: the case of black Pentecostal preaching. In G McGregor & R.S. White (eds) *Reception & Response: Hearer, Creativity and the Analysis of Spoken and Written Texts.* London: Routledge, pp 160-178.

Calley, M. (1965) *God's people: West Indian Pentecostal sects in England.* Oxford: Oxford University Press.

Campbell, H. D. (1979) *The rag doll and other stories.* Kingston Jamaica: Savacou Publications Ltd.

Carby, H (1980) *Multicultural fictions.* Occasional Paper No 58, Centre for Contemporary Cultural Studies. University of Birmingham.

Carrington, L. & Borley, D. (eds) (1977) *The language arts syllabus, 1975. Comment and Countercomment.* University of Saint Augustine, Trinidad.

Cashmore, E. (1979) *Rastaman: the rastafarian movement in England.* London: Allen P. Unwin.

Cassidy, F. & Le. Page, R. (1967) *Jamaica talk.* Cambridge: Cambridge University Press.

Chandler-Harris, J. (1918) *Uncle Remus returns.* Boston.

Christy, P. (1990) Language as expression of identity in Dominica. *International Journal of the Sociology of Language* 85: 61-69.

Coard, B. (1971) *How the West Indian child is made educationally subnormal in the British school system.* London: New Beacon Books.

Commission for Racial Equality (1985) *Birmingham Local Education Authority and schools: referral and suspension of pupils.* London: CRE.

Cones, J. H. (1970) Black consciousness and the Black Church. *Christianity and Crises* 10 (18): 246-246.

Consentino, D. (1982) *Defiant maids and stubborn farmers: tradition and invention in Mende story performances.* Cambridge: Cambridge University Press.

Corson, D. (1993) *Language, minority education and gender.* Clevedon, Avon: Multilingual Matters.

Craton, M. (1982) *Testing the chains: resistance to slavery in the British West Indies.* Ithaca: Cornell University Press.

Crowley, D. (1966) *I could tell old story good: creativity in Bahamian folklore.* Berkeley and Los Angeles: University of California Press.

Dalphinis, M. (1985) *Caribbean and African languages.* London: Karia Press.

Dalphinis, M. (1991) The West African speech communities. In S. Alladina & V. Edwards (eds) *Multilingualism in the British Isles.* London: Longman, 33-55.

Dandy, E. B. (1991) *Black communications: breaking down the barriers.* Chicago Illinois: Afro-American Images.

Davis, G. (1985) *I got the words in me and I can sing it you know.* Philadelphia: University of Pennsylvania.

Dayton, E. (1981) *The social context of be done - a Black English tense aspect marker.* NWAVEX Conference, Philadelphia.

Dayton, E. (1983) *Invariant BE in Black English.* Minneapolis: LSA.

De Rueck, A. &. Knight, J. (eds.) (1967) *Caste and race: comparative approaches.* Boston: Little Brown.

DeBose, C. E. (1992) Code switching: black English and standard English in the African-American linguistic repertoire. *Journal of Multilingual and Multicultural Development 13* (1&2): 157-167.

DeCamp, D. (1961) Social and geographical factors in Jamaican dialects. In R. Le Page &D Decamp. (eds.) *Creole Language Studies 2.* London: Macmillan, 61-84.

DeCamp, D. (1971a) The study of pidgin and creole languages. In D. Hymes (ed.) *Pidginization and creolization of Languages.* Cambridge: Cambridge University Press, pp.13-43.

DeCamp, D. (1971b) Towards a generative analysis of a post-creole speech continuum. In D. Hymes (ed.) *Pidginization and creolization of languages.* Cambridge: Cambridge University Press, 349-70.

Department of Education and Science (DES) (1985) Education for All (The Swann Report). London: H.M.S.O.

Desai, R. (1968) *African society and culture.* New York: M.W. Lads.

Dillard, J. L. (1972) *Black English: its history and usage in the United States.* New York: Random House.

Dillard, J. L. (1992) *A History of American English.* New York: Longman.

Dodd, S. (1993) Down we go. *The Money Index* (351): 46.

Dodgson, E. (1986) *Motherland: West Indian women to Britain in the 1950s.* London: Heinemann Educational Books Ltd.

Dollard, J. (1939) The dozens: dialect of insult. *The American Image* 1: 3-25.

Drew, D. &. Gray, J. (1990) The fifth-year examination achievements of Black young people in England and Wales. *Educational Research* 32 (2): 107-117.

Driver, G. (1980) How West Indians do better at school (especially the girls) *New Society* 17th January: 11-114.

Duckett, D. (1993) *The power of language - a ginger lesson.* Extended essay, B.ed (hons), South Bank University.

Dundes, A., Leach, J. and Ozkok, B. (1972) The strategy of Turkish boys verbal duelling. In J. J. Gumperz & D.Hymes (eds.) *Directions in sociolinguistics: the ethnography of communication.* New York: Holt, Rinehart, Winston, pp.130-60.

Ebony Magazine (1993) *Changing church confronts the changing black family.* Ebony Magazine Vol XlV111.(10) August: 94-100.

Edwards, B. (1973) *The civil and commercial history of the British colonies in the West Indies.* Dublin.

Edwards V. K. & Tomlin C. (1986) *Talking Patois.*In Communication and Education. The Open University EH207.

Edwards, J. (1989) Language and disadvantage. London: Cole and Whurr.

Edwards, J. (1991) (November) Address delivered at *Wedding of Dawn and Ian Lewinson.* New Testament Church of God Wilsden. Bobby G. Videos, 27 Watermead Road, Catford, London SE6.

Edwards, J. (1992) (April) *Jesus Is.* Sermon delivered at De Montfort Hall, Leicester. Sapphire Video Services Ltd. P.O. Box 13 Walsall WS3 1TZ.

Edwards, J. (1992) *Let's praise him again.* London: Kingsway Publications Ltd.

Edwards, J. R. (1979) *Language and disadvantage.* London: Edward Arnold.

Edwards, V. K. (1979) *The West Indian langauge issue in British schools.* London: Routledge & Kegan Paul.

Edwards, V. K. (1983) *Language in multicultural classrooms.* London: Batsford.

Edwards, V. K. (1986) *Language in a Black community.* Clevedon, Avon: Multilingual Matters Ltd.

Edwards, V. K. & Tomlin, C. (1986) *Talking Patois.* Tape accompanying. The Open University course EH207, Communication and Education

Edwards, V. K., Trudgill, P. and Weltens, B. (1984) *The grammar of English dialect: a survey of research.* London: ESRC.

Edwards, V. K. &. Sienkewicz, T. (1990) *Oral cultures past and present: rappin' and Homer.* Oxford: Blackwell.

Edwards, W. (1978) Tantalisin and Busin in Guyana. *Anthropological Linguistics* 20 (5): 194-213.

Edwards, W. F. (1979) The sociolinguistic significance of some Guyanese speech acts. *International Journal of the Sociology of Language* (22): 79-101.

Eggleston, J., Dunn, D. and Anjali, M. (1986) *Education for some: the educational and vocational experiences of 15-18 year old members of minority ethnic groups.* Stoke on Trent: Trentham Books.

Erickson, F. (1984) Rhetoric, anecdote and rhapsody: coherence strategies in a conversation among black American adolescents. In D. Tannen (ed.) *Coherence in spoken and written discourse.* Norwood, New Jersey: Ablex, 81-154.

Figueroa, P. (1982) The West Indian experience. *In Minority experience.* Milton Keynes: The Open University Press pp 29-53.

Finnegan, R. (1967) *Limba stories and storytelling.* Oxford: Clarendon Press.

Finnegan, R. (1970) *Oral literature in Africa.* Oxford: Clarendon Press.

Finnegan, R. (1977) *Oral poetry: its nature, significance and social context.* Cambridge: Cambridge University Press.

Finnegan, R. (1988) *Literacy and orality.* Oxford: Blackwell.

Folb, E. A. (1980) *Runnin down some lines: the language and culture of Black teenagers.* Cambridge, Mass: Harvard University Press.

Foner, N. (1979) *Jamaica farewell: Jamaican migrants in London.* London: Routledge Kegan and Paul.

Foner, P. (1976) *The history of Black Americans: from Africa to the emergence of the cotton kingdom.* Connecticut: Greenwood Press.

Force (1990) *My woman.* Simon music Ltd.

Foster, H. L. (1974) *Ribbin, jivin' and playin' the dozens: the unrecognized dilemma of inner city schools.* Cambridge, Mass: Lippincottt Company.

Foster, M. (1989) "It's cookin' now": a performance analysis of the speech events of a Black teacher in an urban community college. *Language in society* 18 (1): 1-29.

Foster, M. (1991) "Just got to find a way": Case studies of the lives and practice of exemplary Black high school teachers. In. M. Foster (ed.) *Qualitative investigations into schools and schooling.* New York: AMS Press, pp. 273-309.

Fraser, P.(1984) *The contributions of black people to London: some historical reflections.* Paper presented to Conference on the History of Black People in London. Institute of Education: University of London. 27th-29th November 1984

Fryer, P. (1984) *Staying power: the history of black people in Britain.* London: Pluto Press.

Gal, S. (1979) *Language shift: social determinants of linguistic change in bilingual Austria.* New York: Academic Press.

Garvey, A. J. & Essien-Udom E. U.(eds) (1977) *More philosophy and opinions of Marcus Garvey.* London: Frank Cass.

George, C. (1973) *Segregated sabbath: Richard Allen and the rise of independent churches.* New York Open University Press.

George, S. (1975) Girlie girlie. *Jet star Reggae Hits, volume 3.* Sangie Davis Music.

Gerloff, R. (1992) *A plea for British Black theologies: the Black church movement in Britain and its transatlantic cultural and theological interaction with special reference to the Pentecostal oneness (Apostolic) and Sabbatarian movements* (Studies in the intercultural history of Christianity 2 (77). Frankfurt: Verlag Peter Lang.

Giles, H. & Powersland, P. (1975) *Speech styles and social evaluation.* London: Academic Press.

Gold, R. L. (1958) Roles in sociological field work. *Social Forces* 36: 217-23.

Goodman, M. F. (1964) *A comparative study of creole French dialects.* The Hague: Mouton.

Goody, J. & Watt., I. (1968) The consequences of literacy. In J. Goody (ed.) *Literacy in traditional societies.* Cambridge: Cambridge University Press, pp.27-68.

Gordon, J. (1981) *Verbal Deficit: A Critique.* London: Croom Helm.

Hadi, S. (1976) *Some language issues.* Unpublished Paper for a survey undertaken as part of the Schools Council/NFER Education for a Multiracial Society Project.

Hall, R. A. (1961) How pidgin English has evolved. *New Scientist* 9: 413-5.

Hamilton, C. V. (1972) *The Black preacher in America.* New York: William Morrow.

Hammersley, M. & Atkinson, P. (1987) *Ethnography: principles in practice.* London: Tavistock.

Hannerz, U. (1969) *Soulside.* New York: Columbia University Press.

Hansell, M. & Ajirotutu. C.S. (1982) Negotiating interpretations in inter-ethnic settings. In J. Gumperz (ed.) *Language and social Identity.* Cambridge: Cambridge University Press, 85-94.

Hare, N. &. Hare, J. (1985) *Bringing the Black Boy to Manhood.* San Francisco, California: Black Think Tank.

Harris, M. (1964) *Patterns of race in the Americas.* New York: Walker.

Harris, R. (1979) *Caribbean English and adult literacy.* London: ALBSU.

Heath, S. (1982) What no bedtime story means: Narrative skills at home and school. *Language in Society* 11: 49-76.

Heath, S. (1983) *Ways with words: ethnography of communication in communities and classrooms.* Cambridge: Cambridge University Press.

Heath, S. (1988) Protean shapes in literacy events: ever-shifting oral and literate traditions. In D. Tannen (ed.) *Spoken and written language.* Norwood: New Jersey: Ablex, pp.91-117.

Hebdige, R. (1975) Reggae, rastas and rudies. In S Hall &T. Jefferson (eds) *Youth sub-cultures in post-war Britain.* London: Hutchinson, pp.135-54.

Heller, M. (1988) *Codeswitching: anthropological and sociolinguistic perspectives.* Berlin: Mouton de Gruyter.

Henderson, S. (1973) *Understanding the New Black Poetry.* New York: William Morrow.

Henry, I., Joshua, H. & Sargeant, R. (1982) Power, culture and identity: the case of the Afro-Caribbean people. In *Minority Experience.* Milton Keynes: The Open University Press. pp.54-66.

Herskovits, M (1958) *The myth of the Negro Past.* Bost Beacon Press.

Herskovits, M. & Herskovits F.(1958) *Dahomean narrative: a cross-cultural analysis.* Evanston: North Western University Press.

Herskovits, M. (1937) *Suriname folklore.* London: Oxford University Press.

Hewitt, R. (1986) *White talk black talk.* Cambridge: Cambridge University Press.

Hill, C. (1963) *West Indian migrants and the London churches.* Oxford: Oxford University Press.

Hiro, D. (1973) *Black British, White* British. Harmondsworth: Penguin.

HMSO (1991) *Aspects of Britain's ethnic minorities.* London: H.M.S.O.

Hollengweger, W. (1972) *The Pentecostals.* London: S.C.M. Press.

Holloway, J. E. (ed.) (1991) *Africanism in American culture.* Indiana University Press.

Holt , G.S. (1972) 'Stylin' outta the black pulpit. In T. Kochman (ed.) *Rappin and stylin' out in urban Black America.* Champiagn, Urbana: University of Illinois Press, pp.189-204.

Hooks, B. (1993) *Sisters of the yam.* California, L.A.: Turnaround.

Hymes, D. H. (1972) Directions in sociolinguistics: the ethnography of communication. In J. Gumperz & D. Hymes (eds) *Models of interaction of language and social life.* New York: Holt, Rinehart and Winston,

Hymes, D. (1974) *Foundations in sociolinguistic: an ethnographic approach.* Philadelphia: University of Pennyslvania Press.

Idahosa, B. (1988) (May)*Where are you going ?* Sermon delivered at the Kensington Temple. Kensington Park Road London, W11.
Innes, G. (1974) *Sunjata: three Mandinka versions.* London: School of Oriental and African Studies.

Jackson, L. A. (1986) Proverbs of Jamaican. In D. Sutcliffe & A. Wong (eds) *The Language of the Black Experience*. Oxford: Basil Blackwell, pp.

James, C. L. R. (1980) *Fighting racism in world war II.* New York: Monad Press.

Jaynes, G. &. Williams, R. (1989) *A common destiny: blacks and American society.* Washington, D.C: National Academy Press.

Jencks, C. (1975) *Inequality: a reassessment of the effect of family and schooling in America* Harmondsworth: Penguin.

Jensen, A. (1969) How much can we boost I.Q. and scholastic achievement? *Harvard Educational Review* (39): 1-123.

Joda, T. (1989) *The other side of the coin* .Sermon, Voice of Faith Ministries PO Box 3281 S/Lere. Lagos Nigeria.

Junker, B. (1960) *Fieldwork.* Chicago, Ill: University of Chicago Press.

Keddic, N. (1973) *Tinker, Tailor...the myth of cultural deprivation.* Harmondsworth: Penguin Education.

Kernan, K. T., Sodergen, J. & and French, R. (1977) Speech and social prestige in the Belizian speech community. In B G. Blount. & M. Sanches (eds) *Language, thought and culture.* London: Academic Press, pp.35-50.

King, M. L. (1990) *Martin Luther King.* Excerpts of speeches compiled by Peace Pledge Union, Dick Sheppard House, 6 Endsleigh Street London WC1H ODX.

Kochman, T. (1972) Towards an ethnography of Black American speech behaviour. In T. Kochman (ed.) *Rappin' and stylin' out: communication in urban Black America.* Urbana, Illinois: University of Illinois Press, pp.241-64.

Kochman, T. (1981) *Black and white styles in conflict.* Chicago and Illinois: University of Chicago Press.

Kunjufu, J. (1986) *Countering the conspiracy to destroy Black boys.* Chicago, Illinois: African-American Images.

Labov, W. & Harris W A. (1986) De facto segregation of black and white vernaculars. In D. Sankoff (ed.) *Current issues in linguistic theory, diversity and diachrony.* Amsterdam: John Benjamins, pp.1-24.

Labov, W. (1969) The logic of non-standard English. *Monographs on language and linguistics* 22: 1-31.

Labov, W. (1973) The logic of non-standard English. In P. N. Keddie(ed.) *Tinker Tailor: the myth of cultural deprivation.* Harmondsworth: Penguin, pp.21-66.

Labov, W. (1977) *Language in the inner city: studies in the Black English vernacular.* Oxford: Basil Blackwell.

Labov, W. (1987) Are black and white vernaculars diverging? *American Speech* (62): 5-12.

Labov, W., Cohen, Robins, C. & Lewis, J. (1968) *A study of the non-stndard English negro and Puerto-Rican speakers in New York City. Report on cooperative Research Project* 3288. New York: Columbia University.

Ladner, J. (1972) *Tomorrow's tomorrow, the black woman.* New York: Anchor Doubleday.
Ladson-Billings, G. (1991) Returning to the source: implications for educating teachers of black students. In M. Foster (ed.) *Qualitative investigations into schools and schooling.* New York: AMS Press, pp.227-244.

Lawrence, H. G. (1962) *African explorers of the new world.* The Crises June July 159.

Lawton, D. (1980) Language attitude, discreteness and code-shifting in Jamaican Creole. *English Worldwide* 1 (2): 211-26.

Le Page, R. &. Decamp D. (1960) *Jamaican Creole: Creole studies 1.* London: Macmillan.

Leacock, E. (1971) *The Culture of poverty: a critique.* New York: Simon and Schuster.

Levine, L. W. (1977) Black culture and black consciousness. New York: Oxford University Press.

Lieberson, S. (1980) *A piece of the pie.* Berkeley: University of California Press.

Lincoln, E. & Lawrence, H. M. (1990) *The Black church and the African-American experience.* Durham NC: Duke University Press.

Little, A. (1975) The background of under-achievement in immigrant children in London. In G Verma & C.Bagley (eds.) *Race and education across cultures.* London: Heinemann Educational Books Ltd,

Lomax, A. (1970) The homogeneity of Afro-American musical styles. In N. Swzed & J. Whitten (eds) *Afro-American anthropology contemporary perspectives.* New York: Free Press,

Long, E. (1774) *History of Jamaica.* London.

Lord, A. B. (1960) *The singer of tales.* Cambridge MA: Harvard University Press.

Lowenthal, D. (1972) West Indian societies. Oxford: Oxford University Press.

Mabey, C. (1981) Black British literacy: a study of reading attainment of London black children from 8 to 15 years. *Educational Research* 23 (2): 83-95.

MacRoberts,I. (1989) The new Black-led Pentecostal churches in Britain. In P. Badham (ed.) *Religion state and society in modern Britain.* Lampeter: Edwin Mellen Press.pp 119-143.

Marley, B. (1984) No woman, No cry. *Legend of the best of Bob Marley and the Wailers,* Island Records Ltd.

Massey, I. (1991) *More than skin deep: developing anti-racist multicultural education in school.* Sevenoaks, Kent: Hodder & Stoughton.

Matthews, W. (1935) Sailors' pronunciation in the second half of the seventeenth century. *Anglia* (47): 192-251.

Maugham, B. & Rutter, M. (1986) Black pupils progress in secondary school - II examination attainment. *British Journal of Development Psychology* 4: 19-23.

Mbiti, J. (1977) *African religions and philosophy.* Heinemann Educational Press.

McDonald, M. (1989) The exploitation of linguistic mis-match: towards an ethnography of customs and manners. In R. Grillo (ed.) *Social anthroplogy and the politics of language.* London: Routledge & Kegan Paul.

McManus, E. J. (1973) *Black bondage in the North.* New York: Syracuse.

Michael, S. & Collins, J. (1984) Oral discourse style: classroom interaction and the acquisition of literacy. In D. Tannen (ed.) *Coherence in spoken and written discourse.* Norwood: New Jersey: Ablex, pp.219-44.

Michaels, S. & Cazden C. (1986) Teacher child collaboration as oral preparation for literacy. In B. Schiefflein & P. Gilmore (eds) *The acquisition of literacy: ethnographic perspectives.* Norwood, NJ: Ablex, pp.132-154.

Miller, E. (1990) Contemporary issues in Jamaican education. In C. Brock. & D. Clarkson (eds.) *Education in Central America and the Caribbean*. London: Routledge, pp.100-137.

Milner, D. (1983) *Children and race: ten years on*. London: Ward Lock Educational.

Milroy, L. (1980) *Language and social networks*. Oxford: Basil Blackwell.

Mitchell, E. P. (1986) Oral tradition legacy of faith for the Black church. *Religious Education* 81 (1): 93-112.

Mitchell, H. (1970) *Black preaching*. New York: J.B. Hippricott Co.

Mitchell, H. (1990) *Black preaching: the recovery of a powerful art*. Nashville: Abingdon Press.

Morley, J. (1992) Rap music as American history. In A. Stanley (ed.) *Rap the lyrics: the words to rap's greatest hits*. New York: Penguin.

Morris, M. (1983) People speech: some dub poets. *Race Today Review* 14 (5): 150-157.

Morrish, I. (1982) *Obeah, Christ and rastaman*. Cambridge: James Clark.

Mortimore, P., Sammons, P., Stoll, L., Lewis, I. and Ecob, R. (1988) *School matters - the junior years*. Somerset: Open Books.

Murray, R. N. & Gbedemah, G.L. (1983) *Foundations of education in the Caribbean*. London: Hodder and Stoughton.

Nash, J. E. (1991) Race and words: a note on the sociolinguistic divisiveness of race in American Society. *Sociological Inquiry* 61 (2): 252-262.

National Association of Schoolmasters (NAS) (1969) *Education and the immigrants.* Hemel Hempstead, Herts: Educare.

Nicholas, J. (1994) *Language diversity surveys as agents of change.* Clevedon, Avon: Multilingual Matters.

Niles, L. A. (1985) Rhetorical characteristics of traditional Black Preaching. *Journal of Black Studies.* 15 (1): 41-52.

Nketia, J. H. K. (1979) Akan poetry. In U. Beier (ed.) *Introduction to African literature.* London: Longman, Nottinghamshire County Council Education Department (1992) *An enquiry into pupils exclusions from Nottingham secondary schools.* No 15/89 Nottingham: Nottinghamshire County Council Education Department and Advisory and Inspection Service.

O'Callaghan, E. (1981) *A study of Creole in the West Indian novel.* M Litt Oxford: Wolfson College.

Okpewho, I. (1992) *African oral Literature.* Bloomington and Indianapolis: Indiana University Press.

Ong, W. (1978) Literacy and orality in our times. *Association of Departments of English Bulletin* 58 (September): 1-7.

Oosthuizen, G. C. (1979) *Afro-Christian religion.* Holland: State University of Groningen.

Parry, M. (1930) Studies in the epic technique of oral verse-making. In: *Homer and Homeris style.* Harvard Studies in Classical Philogy (41) 73-147.

Patterson, O. (1967) *The Sociology of Slavery.* London: MacGibbon & Kee.

Peach, C (1968) *West Indian migration to Britain: a social geography.* London: Oxford University Press for Institute of Race Relations.

Perera, K. (1984) *Children's writing and reading: analysing classroom language.* Oxford: Blackwell.

Pettigrew, T. (1964) *A profile of the negro American.* Princeston: D. Van Nostrand.

Petyt, M.K. (1970) *Emily Bronte and the haworth dialect* Menston, Yorkshire; Yorkshire Dialect Society.

Piestrup, A. (1974) *Black dialect interference and accommodation of reading instruction in first grade.* Berkeley: University of California.

Pryce, K. (1979) *Endless pressure.* Harmondsworth: Penguin.

Public Enemy (1991) Shut Em down. *Riden, Hour, Depper, Robertz and G Wiz Shut Em down. Apocolypse '91 The Enemy Strikes back.* Sony Music Entertainment Inc.

Rampton, A. (1981) *West Indian children in our schools* (Interim Report of the Committee of Inquiry into the Education of Children from Ethnic Minority Groups. London: HMSO.

Rees, B. & Sherwood M. (1992) *Black peoples of the Americas.* Oxford: Heinemann Educational.

Reisman, K. (1970) Cultural and linguistic ambiguity in a West Indian village. In N. Swzed & J Whitten (eds.) *Afro-American Anthropology: Contemporary Perspectives.* New York: Free Press, pp.129-44.

Reisman, K. (1974) Contrapuntal conversations in an Antiguan village. In R Bauman & J.Sherzer (ed.) *Exploration in the ethnography of speaking.* Cambridge: Cambridge University Press, pp.110-24.

Roberts, P. A. (1988) *West Indians and their language.* Cambridge: Cambridge University Press.

Rolle, U. (1988) *Your God is a jealous God.* Ulrich Rolle Ministries PO Box, Miami: Florida.

Romaine, S. (1988) *Pidgin and creole languages.* New York: Longman.

Rosen, H.&. Burgess, T. (1980) *Languages and dialects of London school children.* London: Ward Lock Educational.

Rosenberg B.A.(1988) *Can these bones live: the art of the American folk preacher.* Chicago: University of Illinois Press.

Rosenberg, M. (1979) *Conceiving the self.* New York: Basic Books.

Saa, S. (1985) *Jamaican Creole: to what extent it impedes the achievement of West Indian pupils in the Secondary School.* B.ed. (hons) dissertation. West Midlands College of Higher Education.
Salt & Pepa (1988) *A salt with a deadly pepa.* Channel 5, Next Plateau Records Inc.

Samuda, R. J. (1975) *Psychological testing of American minorities: issues and consequences.* New York: Harper and Row.
Saville-Troike, M. (1982) *The ethnography of communication.* Oxford: Basil Blackwell.

Sebba, M. (1993) *London Jamaican.* London: Longman.

Shorter, A. (1974) *African culture and the Christian church.* London: Macmillan Education Ltd.

Shuy, R. W. and Riley, W. (1968) *Field techniques in urban language study.* Washington, D.C: Center for Applied Linguistics.
Simpson, G. E. (1978) *Black religions in the new world:* New York: Columbia University Press.

Singana, S. and Ipi 'N Tombia (1973) *The Digger.* MVN Studios, John Lindman.

Smawfield, D. (1990) Education in the British Virgin Islands: case study of a Caribbean micro state. In C. Brock & D. Clarkson (eds) *Education in Central America and the Caribbean.* London: Routledge, pp 138-173.

Smitherman, G. (1977) *Talkin' and testifyin': the language of Black America.* Boston: Houghton Mifflin Co.

Smitherman, G. (1992) Black English, diverging or converging? The view from the national assessment of educational progress. *Language and Education* 6 (1): 48-60.

Spears, A. (1987) Are black and white vernaculars diverging? *American Speech* 62 (1): 48-55.

Spillers, H. (1971) Martin Luther King and the style of the black sermon. *The Black Scholar* (September): 14-27.

Stone, M. (1981) *The education of the black child in Britain: the myth of multiracial education.* London: Fontana.

Sullivan, J. P. (1980) The validity of literary dialect: evidence from the theatrical portrayal of Hiberno-English forms. *Language in Society* 9 (2): 195-219.

Supercat (1992) *Don dadda.* Sony Music Entertainment Inc.

Sutcliffe, D. (1978) *The language of the first and second generation West Indian children in Bedfordshire.* M.Ed. thesis, University of Leicester.

Sutcliffe, D. & Tomlin, C. (1986) The Black churches. In D. Sutcliffe & A. Wong (eds.) *The Language of the black experience.* Oxford: Basil Blackwell, pp.15-31.

Sutcliffe, D. (1982) *British Black English.* Oxford: Basil Blackwell.

Sutcliffe, D. (1992) *System in Black language*. Avon: Multilingual Matters Ltd.

Synan, V. (1975) *The holiness Pentecostal movement in the United States*. Michigan: Grand Rapids.

Tanna, L (1984) *Jamaican folk tales and oral histories*. Kingston: Institute of Jamaica Publications.

Tannen, D (1989) *Talking voices: repetition, dialogue and imagery in conversational discourse*. Cambridge: Cambridge University Press.

Tannen, D. (1980a) Oral literate strategies in discourse. *Linguistic Reporter* 22 (9): 1-3.

Tannen, D. (1988) Oral versus literate tradition. In D. Tannen (ed.) *Spoken and written language*. Norwood: New Jersey: Ablex, pp.1-16.

Taylor, O.L.(1975) Black language and what to do about it: some black community perspectives. In R. L. Williams (ed.) *Ebonics: the true language of black folks*. St. Louis: Institute of Black Studies, pp. 29-39.

The Economist (1991a) America's wasted Blacks and America's Blacks: a world apart. *The Economist* **30 March: 3-14 & 21-23.**
The Economist (1991b) America's Blacks. *The Economist* 30 March:21-2.

Thompson, R. F. (1974) *African art in motion*. Los Angeles: University of California Press.

Todd, L. (1984) *Modern Englishes: pidgins and creoles*. Oxford. Basil Blackwell.

Todd, L. (1974) *Pidgins and creoles*. London: Routledge and Kegan Paul Ltd.

Tomlin C. (1988) *Black preaching style.* M Phil Thesis. Birmingham: University of Birmingham.

Tomlin. C. (1981) *To what extent do linguistic differences hinder or enhance learning: a study of the West Indian Language.* Unpublished Special Study, Dudley College of Higher Education.

Tomlinson, S. (1984) *Home and school in multicultural Britain.* London: Batsford.

Toop, D. (1984) *The rap attack: African jive to New York hip hop.* London: Pluto Press Ltd.

Townsend, H. (1971) *Immigrants in England: the LEA response.* Windsor: National Foundation for Educational Research.

Troyna, B. & Smith D.I. (eds) (1983) *Racism, school and the labour market.* Leicester: National Youth Bureau.

Troyna, B. (1979) Differential commitment to ethnic identity by black youths in Britain. *New Community* 7: 406-14.

Turner, L. D. (1949) *Africanisms in the Gullah dialect.* Ann Arbor: University of Michigan Press.

Turner, R.D. (1991) First ladies of rap. *Ebony* . XLVI (12): 58-60. Vaughn-Cooke, F. (1987) Are black and white vernaculars diverging? *American Speech* (65): 62-72.

Walvin, J. (1984) *Passage to Britain.* Harmondsworth Pelican. Walvin, J. (1992) *Black ivory: a history of British slavery.* London: Harper Collins.

Warner-Lewis M(1979) The African impact on language and literature in the English-speaking Caribbean. Continued existence of African languages: a case study of Yoruba in Trinidad. In M. E. Graham. & F. W. Knight (eds.) *Africa and the Caribbean: The legacies of a link.* Baltimore and London: John Hopkins University Press, pp.100-121.

Watson, G. L. (1991) *Jamaican sayings, notes on folklore aesthetics and social control.* Tallahassee: Florida A.P.M. University Press.

Weinberg, M. (1977) *Minority students: a research appraisal.* Washington D.C: National Institute of Education.

Wilkinson, J. L. (1993) *Church in black and white: the black christian tradition in 'mainstream' churches in England, a white response and testimony.* Edinburgh: Saint Andrew Press.

Wilmore, G.S. (1989) (ed) *African American religious studies.* Durham NC: Duke University Press

Wilson, W. J. (1980) *The declining significance of race: blacks and changing American institutions.* Chicago: University of Chicago Press.

Wilson, W. J. (1987) *The truly disadvantaged: the inner city.* Chicago: University of Chicago Press.

Wolfram, W. (1969) *A sociolinguistic description of Detroit negro speech.* Washington D.C: Centre for Applied Linguistics.

Wolfram, W. (1987) Are black and white vernaculars diverging? *American Speech* 62 (1): 40-48.

Yekwai, D. (1988) British racism: miseducation of the African child. London: Karnak House.

Audio tapes

Callendar, C. & Humphrey, C. (1991) *The art of insult.* Interview with Atilla the Stockbroker. Radio 4 SLN11791FQOO73.

Edwards, V. K. & Tomlin, C. (1986) *Talking Patois.* Tape accompanying The Open University course EH207, Communication and Education

Idahosa, B. (1988) (May)*Where are you going* ? Sermon delivered at the Kensington Temple. Kensington Park Road London, W11.
Joda, T. (1989) *The other side of the coin.* Sermon, Voice of Faith Ministries, PO Box 3281 S/Lere. Lagos Nigeria.

King, M. L. (1990) *Martin Luther King.* Excerpts of speeches compiled by Peace Pledge Union, Dick Sheppard House, 6 Endsleigh Street London WC1H ODX.

Rolle, U. (1988) *Your God is a jealous God.* Ulrich Rolle Ministries PO Box, Miami: Florida.

Salt & Pepa (1988) *A salt with a deadly pepa.* Channel 5, Next Plateau Records Inc.

Video tapes

Blair, Rev. (1990) *Marathana.* Sermon delivered at De Montfort Hall, Leicester. Sapphire Video Services Ltd P.O Box 13 Walsall WS3 1TZ

Edwards, J. (1991) (November) Address delivered at *Wedding of Dawn and Ian Lewinson.* New Testament Church of God Wilsden. Bobby G. Videos, 27 Watermead Road, Catford, London SE6.

Edwards, J. (1992) (April) *Jesus Is.* Sermon delivered at De Monfort Hall, Leicester. Sapphire Video Services.

Records

Aswad (1988) Don't turn around *Island Records.*

Force (1990) *My woman.* Simon music Ltd.

George, S. (1985) Girlie girlie. *Jet star Reggae Hits, volume 3.* Sangie Davis Music.

Marley, B. (1984) No woman, No cry. *Legend of the best of Bob Marley and the Wailers,* Island Records Ltd.

Public Enemy (1991) Shut Em down. *Riden, Hour, Depper, Robertz and G Wiz Shut Em down. Apocolypse '91 The Enemy Strikes back.* Sony Music Entertainment Inc.

Singana, M. and Ipi 'N Tombia (1973) *The Digger.* MVN Studios, John Lindman.

Supercat (1992) *Don dadda.* Sony Music Entertainment Inc.